**GENERAL APTITUDE
AND ABILITIES SERIES**

THIS IS YOUR **PASSBOOK®** FOR ...

VERBAL AND CLERICAL ABILITIES

NLC®

NATIONAL LEARNING CORPORATION®
passbooks.com

Copyright © 2020 by

National Learning Corporation

212 Michael Drive, Syosset, NY 11791
(516) 921-8888 • www.passbooks.com
E-mail: info@passbooks.com

PUBLISHED IN THE UNITED STATES OF AMERICA

PASSBOOK® SERIES

THE *PASSBOOK® SERIES* has been created to prepare applicants and candidates for the ultimate academic battlefield – the examination room.

At some time in our lives, each and every one of us may be required to take an examination – for validation, matriculation, admission, qualification, registration, certification, or licensure.

Based on the assumption that every applicant or candidate has met the basic formal educational standards, has taken the required number of courses, and read the necessary texts, the *PASSBOOK® SERIES* furnishes the one special preparation which may assure passing with confidence, instead of failing with insecurity. Examination questions – together with answers – are furnished as the basic vehicle for study so that the mysteries of the examination and its compounding difficulties may be eliminated or diminished by a sure method.

This book is meant to help you pass your examination provided that you qualify and are serious in your objective.

The entire field is reviewed through the huge store of content information which is succinctly presented through a provocative and challenging approach – the question-and-answer method.

A climate of success is established by furnishing the correct answers at the end of each test.

You soon learn to recognize types of questions, forms of questions, and patterns of questioning. You may even begin to anticipate expected outcomes.

You perceive that many questions are repeated or adapted so that you can gain acute insights, which may enable you to score many sure points.

You learn how to confront new questions, or types of questions, and to attack them confidently and work out the correct answers.

You note objectives and emphases, and recognize pitfalls and dangers, so that you may make positive educational adjustments.

Moreover, you are kept fully informed in relation to new concepts, methods, practices, and directions in the field.

You discover that you arre actually taking the examination all the time: you are preparing for the examination by "taking" an examination, not by reading extraneous and/or supererogatory textbooks.

In short, this PASSBOOK®, used directedly, should be an important factor in helping you to pass your test.

VERBAL ABILITIES TEST

DIRECTIONS AND SAMPLE QUESTIONS

Study the sample questions carefully. Each question has four suggested answers. Decide which one is the best answer. Find the question number on the Sample Answer Sheet. Show your answer to the question by darkening completely the space corresponding to the letter that is the same as the letter of your answer. Keep your mark within the space. If you have to erase a mark, be sure to erase it completely. Mark only one answer for each question. Do NOT mark space E for any question.

SAMPLE VERBAL QUESTIONS

I. *Previous* means most nearly

    A. abandoned   C. timely
    B. former   D. younger

II. *(Reading)* "Just as the procedure of a collection department must be clear cut and definite, the steps being taken with the sureness of a skilled chess player, so the various paragraphs of a collection letter must show clear organization, giving evidence of a mind that, from the beginning, has had a specific end in view."
The quotation best supports the statement that a collection letter should always

    A. show a spirit of sportsmanship
    B. be divided into several paragraphs
    C. be brief, but courteous
    D. be carefully planned

III. Decide which sentence is preferable with respect to grammar and usage suitable for a formal letter or report.

    A. They do not ordinarily present these kind of reports in detail like this.
    B. A report of this kind is not hardly ever given in such detail as this one.
    C. This report is more detailed than what such reports ordinarily are.
    D. A report of this kind is not ordinarily presented in as much detail as this one is.

IV. Find the correct spelling of the word and darken the proper answer space. If no suggested spelling is correct, darken space D.

    A. athalete   C. athlete
    B. athelete   D. none of these

V. SPEEDOMETER is related to POINTER as WATCH is related to

    A. case   C. dial
    B. hands   D. numerals

CLERICAL ABILITIES TESTS

This guide provides a general description of the subject areas to be tested and the different types of questions you will likely see on any of the tests in this series. The Examination Announcement will specify the exact subject areas to be included on the specific test you will be taking.

The Clerical Abilities Tests have an overall time allowance of 3 hours. They are divided into five subject areas and the questions are designed to evaluate the following abilities:

1. SPELLING: These questions test your ability to spell words that are used in written business communications.
2. ALPHABETIZING: These questions test your ability to file material in alphabetical order.
3. RECORD KEEPING: These questions evaluate your ability to perform common record keeping tasks. The test consists of two or more "sets" of questions; each set concerning a different problem. Typical record keeping problems might involve the organization or collation of data from several sources; scheduling; maintaining a record system using running balances; or completion of a table summarizing data using totals, subtotals, averages and percents.
4. CLERICAL OPERATIONS WITH LETTERS AND NUMBERS: These questions test your skills and abilities in clerical operations involving alphabetizing, comparing, checking and counting. The questions require you to follow the specific directions given for each question which may involve alphabetizing, comparing, checking and counting given groups of letters and/or numbers.
5. USING A DIRECTORY: These questions test your ability to keep directory records and to supply accurate information to callers. The questions require you to incorporate name and/or room changes into a current telephone directory and to answer questions, such as those that would be asked by callers, about the information contained in the directory listing.

The Examination Announcement will list two or more of the above subject areas to be included in the written test you will be taking. All written tests in the series include CLERICAL OPERATIONS WITH LETTERS AND NUMBERS.

The remainder of this guide explains how you are tested in each of these subject areas. A **TEST TASK** is provided for each subject. This is an explanation of how a question is presented and how to correctly answer it. Be sure to read each one carefully.

You will also be given at least one **SAMPLE QUESTION** for each subject area. It will be of the type that you will see on the actual test. The **SOLUTION** and correct answer are provided after each question. You should study the question and its solution until you understand how it works.

SUBJECT AREA 1

SPELLING: These questions test you ability to spell words that are used in written business communications.

TEST TASK: You are given questions that contain a list of words. You must determine which, if any, of the words is misspelled.

SAMPLE QUESTION:

Which one of the following words is misspelled?
A. manageable
B. circumstants
C. legality
D. None of the above is misspelled

The answer is B.

SOLUTION: *To answer this question, you must examine each of the words. The words "manageable" (choice A) and "legality" (choice C) are spelled correctly. The word "circumstants" (choice B) is misspelled. The correct spelling is "circumstance."*

SUBJECT AREA 2

ALPHABETIZING: These questions test your ability to file material in alphabetical order.

TEST TASK: You will be provided with a list of names. You must put the names into alphabetical order.

SAMPLE QUESTION:

Of the following, which one should be THIRD in an alphabetical file?
A. Docker, John
B. Decker, Jane
C. Dinckman, June
D. Dockman, James

The answer is A.

SOLUTION: *To answer this question, you must first put the names into alphabetical order. "Decker, Jane" would be first. "Dinckman, June" would be second. "Docker, John" would be third followed by "Dockman, James." The question asks for the third name on the list. The answer is "Docker, John" (choice A).*

SUBJECT AREA 3

RECORD KEEPING: These questions test your ability to perform common record keeping tasks.

TEST TASK: The questions in this subject area are contained in two or more sets. Each set presents a different problem. Typical record keeping problems might involve:
- organization or collation of data from several sources
- scheduling
- maintaining a record system using running balances
- completion of a table summarizing data using totals, subtotals, averages and percents

SAMPLE QUESTIONS:

The following two questions are based on the table below.

NUMBER OF AUTOMOBILE ACCIDENTS BY LOCATION AND CAUSE (1998)				
	LOCATION 1		LOCATION 2	
CAUSE	Number	Percent	Number	Percent
Road Conditions	10	20	25	42
Drunk Drivers	20	40	5	8
Speeding	15	30	15	25
Unknown	5	10	15	25
TOTALS	50	100	60	100

QUESTION 1: Which of the following is the SECOND highest cause of accidents for both locations combined?
- A. Road Conditions
- B. Drunk Drivers
- C. Speeding
- D. Unknown

The answer is C

SOLUTION: *To answer this question, you must first add the number from location 1 to the number from location 2 for each accident cause. Then, you must rank the causes from highest to lowest based on the totals you obtain. You can then determine the second highest cause of accidents for both locations combined. In this example, "Road Conditions" (choice A) would be the highest cause of accidents with 35. The second highest cause of accidents is "Speeding" (choice C) with 30. The correct answer is "Speeding" (choice C).*

QUESTION 2: The average number of automobile accidents per week that occurred in Location 2 in 1998 (52 weeks) was most nearly
- A. 0.8
- B. 1.2
- C. 2.1
- D. 5.2

The answer is B

SOLUTION: *To answer this question, you must divide the total number of accidents in location 2 (60), by 52 weeks. The answer, rounded to the nearest tenth is 1.2 (choice B).*

SUBJECT AREA 4

CLERICAL OPERATIONS WITH LETTERS AND NUMBERS: These questions test your skills and abilities in clerical operations involving alphabetizing, comparing, checking and counting. The questions require you to follow the specific directions given for each question which may involve alphabetizing, comparing, checking and counting given groups of letters and/or numbers.

TEST TASK: You are given questions, which require you to follow specific directions given for each question. Each question may involve alphabetizing, comparing, checking and counting given groups of letters and/or numbers.

SAMPLE QUESTIONS:

QUESTION 1: How many pairs of the following groups of letters are exactly alike?

BRFQSX	BRFQSX
ACDOBJ	ACDBOJ
RPTQVS	RPTQVS
ZUYRVB	ZUYRVB
SPQRAS	SQRPAS
HVCBWR	HVCRWB

A. 2
B. 3
C. 4
D. 5

The answer is B.

SOLUTION: *To answer this question you must compare the column of letter groups on the left to the column of letter groups on the right. BRFQSX, RPTQVS and ZUYRVB of the left column are exactly like BRFQSX, RPTQVS and ZUYRVB of the right column. The other groups of letters are not exactly alike so the answer is 3 (choice B).*

QUESTION 2: In the following sentence, how many words contain letters that appear more than once in that word?

"Right around April Fool's Day, the daffodils and crocuses start to emerge and cheer us up after a long winter."

A. 5
B. 6
C. 7
D. 8

The answer is B.

SOLUTION: *To answer this question, look at each word to see how many contain the same letter at least twice. The words that do are: "Fool's," "daffodils," "crocuses," "start," "emerge," and "cheer." The total number of words is 6. The answer is 6 (choice B).*

SUBJECT AREA 4 (cont.)

QUESTION 3: Which one of the following letters is as far after C as T is after O in the alphabet?

    A. G
    B. H
    C. I
    D. J

The answer is B.

SOLUTION: *Count how many letters are between O and T in the alphabet. There are 4: P, Q, R and S. There are also 4 letters between C and H: D, E, F and G. The answer is H (choice B).*

QUESTION 4: In the following list of numbers, how many times does 8 come just after 6 when 6 comes just after an odd number?

          6325687253494236844576842396868

    A. 2
    B. 3
    C. 4
    D. 5

The answer is C.

SOLUTION: *To answer this question, you must determine the number of times 8 follows 6 when 6 follows an odd number. There are 4 occasions where 8 follows 6 and the number 6 follows an odd number. They are 568, 368, 768 and 968. The answer is 4 (choice C).*

SUBJECT AREA 5

USING A DIRECTORY: These questions test your ability to keep directory records and to supply accurate information to callers.

TEST TASK: You will be provided with a telephone directory and a list of changes, and you will be asked to incorporate name and/or room changes into the directory. You will be asked to answer questions such as those that would be asked by callers about the information contained in the directory listing.

SAMPLE QUESTION:

Example: This question is based on the DIRECTORY and LIST OF CHANGES shown below:

DIRECTORY

NAME	RM. NO.	EXT.	NAME	RM. NO.	EXT.
Adams, Dave	123	1234	Charles, Bob	126	9109
Brown, Bill	125	5678	Davis, Ann	128	1112
Brull, Betty	142	5768	Diaz, Angel	134	2212
Calvin, Ed	155	2314	Evans, Sue	127	9502
Cerra, Lisa	116	4312	Frank, Chris	151	3456

LIST OF CHANGES in effect today:

All calls for persons not listed above should be referred to Ann Davis in Personnel.

Bill Brown is on vacation; his calls should be referred to Dave Adams whose extension has been changed to 8737.

QUESTION: To which one of the following extensions should a call for Marc Evans be directed?

       A. 1112
       B. 1234
       C. 5678
       D. 8737

Answer is A.

SOLUTION: *To answer this question, you must first determine that Marc Adams is not listed in the directory above, and that calls for people not so listed should be referred to Ann Davis in Personnel. Find Ann Davis in the directory; her extension is 1112 (choice A).*

CONCLUSION

You and your feelings about tests have a great deal to do with how you perform on a test. Some people get so tense and nervous that they don't do as well as they could. They forget things they know or make simple mistakes. The following suggestions should help you overcome these problems.

- Study and review this Guide to become familiar with the test contents.
- Give yourself plenty of time to do what you need to do before the test starts. Arrive at the test room a little ahead of the starting time.
- Try to relax just before the test starts.
- Listen carefully to the instructions the Monitors give you. Carefully read all instructions on the Candidate Directions you are given at the test as well as information on the covers of the test booklets.
- Try to keep calm, cool and collected throughout the test.
- Keep track of time.

HOW TO TAKE A TEST

You have studied long, hard and conscientiously.

With your official admission card in hand, and your heart pounding, you have been admitted to the examination room.

You note that there are several hundred other applicants in the examination room waiting to take the same test.

They all appear to be equally well prepared.

You know that nothing but your best effort will suffice. The "moment of truth" is at hand: you now have to demonstrate objectively, in writing, your knowledge of content and your understanding of subject matter.

You are fighting the most important battle of your life—to pass and/or score high on an examination which will determine your career and provide the economic basis for your livelihood.

What extra, special things should you know and should you do in taking the examination?

I. YOU MUST PASS AN EXAMINATION

A. WHAT EVERY CANDIDATE SHOULD KNOW
Examination applicants often ask us for help in preparing for the written test. What can I study in advance? What kinds of questions will be asked? How will the test be given? How will the papers be graded?

B. HOW ARE EXAMS DEVELOPED?
Examinations are carefully written by trained technicians who are specialists in the field known as "psychological measurement," in consultation with recognized authorities in the field of work that the test will cover. These experts recommend the subject matter areas or skills to be tested; only those knowledges or skills important to your success on the job are included. The most reliable books and source materials available are used as references. Together, the experts and technicians judge the difficulty level of the questions.

Test technicians know how to phrase questions so that the problem is clearly stated. Their ethics do not permit "trick" or "catch" questions. Questions may have been tried out on sample groups, or subjected to statistical analysis, to determine their usefulness.

Written tests are often used in combination with performance tests, ratings of training and experience, and oral interviews. All of these measures combine to form the best-known means of finding the right person for the right job.

II. HOW TO PASS THE WRITTEN TEST

A. BASIC STEPS

1) Study the announcement

How, then, can you know what subjects to study? Our best answer is: "Learn as much as possible about the class of positions for which you've applied." The exam will test the knowledge, skills and abilities needed to do the work.

Your most valuable source of information about the position you want is the official exam announcement. This announcement lists the training and experience qualifications. Check these standards and apply only if you come reasonably close to meeting them. Many jurisdictions preview the written test in the exam announcement by including a section called "Knowledge and Abilities Required," "Scope of the Examination," or some similar heading. Here you will find out specifically what fields will be tested.

2) Choose appropriate study materials

If the position for which you are applying is technical or advanced, you will read more advanced, specialized material. If you are already familiar with the basic principles of your field, elementary textbooks would waste your time. Concentrate on advanced textbooks and technical periodicals. Think through the concepts and review difficult problems in your field.

These are all general sources. You can get more ideas on your own initiative, following these leads. For example, training manuals and publications of the government agency which employs workers in your field can be useful, particularly for technical and professional positions. A letter or visit to the government department involved may result in more specific study suggestions, and certainly will provide you with a more definite idea of the exact nature of the position you are seeking.

3) Study this book!

III. KINDS OF TESTS

Tests are used for purposes other than measuring knowledge and ability to perform specified duties. For some positions, it is equally important to test ability to make adjustments to new situations or to profit from training. In others, basic mental abilities not dependent on information are essential. Questions which test these things may not appear as pertinent to the duties of the position as those which test for knowledge and information. Yet they are often highly important parts of a fair examination. For very general questions, it is almost impossible to help you direct your study efforts. What we can do is to point out some of the more common of these general abilities needed in public service positions and describe some typical questions.

1) General information

Broad, general information has been found useful for predicting job success in some kinds of work. This is tested in a variety of ways, from vocabulary lists to questions about current events. Basic background in some field of work, such as sociology or economics, may be sampled in a group of questions. Often these are principles which have become familiar to most persons through exposure rather than through formal training. It is difficult to advise you how to study for these questions; being alert to the world around you is our best suggestion.

2) Verbal ability

An example of an ability needed in many positions is verbal or language ability. Verbal ability is, in brief, the ability to use and understand words. Vocabulary and grammar tests are typical measures of this ability. Reading comprehension or paragraph interpretation questions are common in many kinds of civil service tests. You are given a paragraph of written material and asked to find its central meaning.

IV. KINDS OF QUESTIONS

1. Multiple-choice Questions

Most popular of the short-answer questions is the "multiple choice" or "best answer" question. It can be used, for example, to test for factual knowledge, ability to solve problems or judgment in meeting situations found at work.

A multiple-choice question is normally one of three types:

- It can begin with an incomplete statement followed by several possible endings. You are to find the one ending which *best* completes the statement, although some of the others may not be entirely wrong.
- It can also be a complete statement in the form of a question which is answered by choosing one of the statements listed.
- It can be in the form of a problem – again you select the best answer.

Here is an example of a multiple-choice question with a discussion which should give you some clues as to the method for choosing the right answer:

When an employee has a complaint about his assignment, the action which will *best* help him overcome his difficulty is to
   A. discuss his difficulty with his coworkers
   B. take the problem to the head of the organization
   C. take the problem to the person who gave him the assignment
   D. say nothing to anyone about his complaint

In answering this question, you should study each of the choices to find which is best. Consider choice "A" – Certainly an employee may discuss his complaint with fellow employees, but no change or improvement can result, and the complaint remains unresolved. Choice "B" is a poor choice since the head of the organization probably does not know what assignment you have been given, and taking your problem to him is known as "going over the head" of the supervisor. The supervisor, or person who made the assignment, is the person who can clarify it or correct any injustice. Choice "C" is, therefore, correct. To say nothing, as in choice "D," is unwise. Supervisors have and interest in knowing the problems employees are facing, and the employee is seeking a solution to his problem.

2. True/False

3. Matching Questions
Matching an answer from a column of choices within another column.

V. RECORDING YOUR ANSWERS

Computer terminals are used more and more today for many different kinds of exams.

For an examination with very few applicants, you may be told to record your answers in the test booklet itself. Separate answer sheets are much more common. If this separate answer sheet is to be scored by machine – and this is often the case – it is highly important that you mark your answers correctly in order to get credit.

VI. BEFORE THE TEST

YOUR PHYSICAL CONDITION IS IMPORTANT
If you are not well, you can't do your best work on tests. If you are half asleep, you can't do your best either. Here are some tips:

1) Get about the same amount of sleep you usually get. Don't stay up all night before the test, either partying or worrying—DON'T DO IT!
2) If you wear glasses, be sure to wear them when you go to take the test. This goes for hearing aids, too.
3) If you have any physical problems that may keep you from doing your best, be sure to tell the person giving the test. If you are sick or in poor health, you relay cannot do your best on any test. You can always come back and take the test some other time.

Common sense will help you find procedures to follow to get ready for an examination. Too many of us, however, overlook these sensible measures. Indeed, nervousness and fatigue have been found to be the most serious reasons why applicants fail to do their best on civil service tests. Here is a list of reminders:

- Begin your preparation early – Don't wait until the last minute to go scurrying around for books and materials or to find out what the position is all about.
- Prepare continuously – An hour a night for a week is better than an all-night cram session. This has been definitely established. What is more, a night a week for a month will return better dividends than crowding your study into a shorter period of time.
- Locate the place of the exam – You have been sent a notice telling you when and where to report for the examination. If the location is in a different town or otherwise unfamiliar to you, it would be well to inquire the best route and learn something about the building.
- Relax the night before the test – Allow your mind to rest. Do not study at all that night. Plan some mild recreation or diversion; then go to bed early and get a good night's sleep.
- Get up early enough to make a leisurely trip to the place for the test – This way unforeseen events, traffic snarls, unfamiliar buildings, etc. will not upset you.

- Dress comfortably – A written test is not a fashion show. You will be known by number and not by name, so wear something comfortable.
- Leave excess paraphernalia at home – Shopping bags and odd bundles will get in your way. You need bring only the items mentioned in the official notice you received; usually everything you need is provided. Do not bring reference books to the exam. They will only confuse those last minutes and be taken away from you when in the test room.
- Arrive somewhat ahead of time – If because of transportation schedules you must get there very early, bring a newspaper or magazine to take your mind off yourself while waiting.
- Locate the examination room – When you have found the proper room, you will be directed to the seat or part of the room where you will sit. Sometimes you are given a sheet of instructions to read while you are waiting. Do not fill out any forms until you are told to do so; just read them and be prepared.
- Relax and prepare to listen to the instructions
- If you have any physical problem that may keep you from doing your best, be sure to tell the test administrator. If you are sick or in poor health, you really cannot do your best on the exam. You can come back and take the test some other time.

VII. AT THE TEST

The day of the test is here and you have the test booklet in your hand. The temptation to get going is very strong. Caution! There is more to success than knowing the right answers. You must know how to identify your papers and understand variations in the type of short-answer question used in this particular examination. Follow these suggestions for maximum results from your efforts:

1) Cooperate with the monitor
The test administrator has a duty to create a situation in which you can be as much at ease as possible. He will give instructions, tell you when to begin, check to see that you are marking your answer sheet correctly, and so on. He is not there to guard you, although he will see that your competitors do not take unfair advantage. He wants to help you do your best.

2) Listen to all instructions
Don't jump the gun! Wait until you understand all directions. In most civil service tests you get more time than you need to answer the questions. So don't be in a hurry. Read each word of instructions until you clearly understand the meaning. Study the examples, listen to all announcements and follow directions. Ask questions if you do not understand what to do.

3) Identify your papers
Civil service exams are usually identified by number only. You will be assigned a number; you must not put your name on your test papers. Be sure to copy your number correctly. Since more than one exam may be given, copy your exact examination title.

4) Plan your time
Unless you are told that a test is a "speed" or "rate of work" test, speed itself is usually not important. Time enough to answer all the questions will be provided, but this

does not mean that you have all day. An overall time limit has been set. Divide the total time (in minutes) by the number of questions to determine the approximate time you have for each question.

5) Do not linger over difficult questions

If you come across a difficult question, mark it with a paper clip (useful to have along) and come back to it when you have been through the booklet. One caution if you do this – be sure to skip a number on your answer sheet as well. Check often to be sure that you have not lost your place and that you are marking in the row numbered the same as the question you are answering.

6) Read the questions

Be sure you know what the question asks! Many capable people are unsuccessful because they failed to *read* the questions correctly.

7) Answer all questions

Unless you have been instructed that a penalty will be deducted for incorrect answers, it is better to guess than to omit a question.

8) Speed tests

It is often better NOT to guess on speed tests. It has been found that on timed tests people are tempted to spend the last few seconds before time is called in marking answers at random – without even reading them – in the hope of picking up a few extra points. To discourage this practice, the instructions may warn you that your score will be "corrected" for guessing. That is, a penalty will be applied. The incorrect answers will be deducted from the correct ones, or some other penalty formula will be used.

9) Review your answers

If you finish before time is called, go back to the questions you guessed or omitted to give them further thought. Review other answers if you have time.

10) Return your test materials

If you are ready to leave before others have finished or time is called, take ALL your materials to the monitor and leave quietly. Never take any test material with you. The monitor can discover whose papers are not complete, and taking a test booklet may be grounds for disqualification.

VIII. EXAMINATION TECHNIQUES

1) Read the general instructions carefully. These are usually printed on the first page of the exam booklet. As a rule, these instructions refer to the timing of the examination; the fact that you should not start work until the signal and must stop work at a signal, etc. If there are any *special* instructions, such as a choice of questions to be answered, make sure that you note this instruction carefully.

2) When you are ready to start work on the examination, that is as soon as the signal has been given, read the instructions to each question booklet, underline any key words or phrases, such as *least, best, outline, describe*

and the like. In this way you will tend to answer as requested rather than discover on reviewing your paper that you *listed without describing*, that you selected the *worst* choice rather than the *best* choice, etc.

3) If the examination is of the objective or multiple-choice type – that is, each question will also give a series of possible answers: A, B, C or D, and you are called upon to select the best answer and write the letter next to that answer on your answer paper – it is advisable to start answering each question in turn. There may be anywhere from 50 to 100 such questions in the three or four hours allotted and you can see how much time would be taken if you read through all the questions before beginning to answer any. Furthermore, if you come across a question or group of questions which you know would be difficult to answer, it would undoubtedly affect your handling of all the other questions.

4) If the examination is of the essay type and contains but a few questions, it is a moot point as to whether you should read all the questions before starting to answer any one. Of course, if you are given a choice – say five out of seven and the like – then it is essential to read all the questions so you can eliminate the two that are most difficult. If, however, you are asked to answer all the questions, there may be danger in trying to answer the easiest one first because you may find that you will spend too much time on it. The best technique is to answer the first question, then proceed to the second, etc.

5) Time your answers. Before the exam begins, write down the time it started, then add the time allowed for the examination and write down the time it must be completed, then divide the time available somewhat as follows:
   - If 3-1/2 hours are allowed, that would be 210 minutes. If you have 80 objective-type questions, that would be an average of 2-1/2 minutes per question. Allow yourself no more than 2 minutes per question, or a total of 160 minutes, which will permit about 50 minutes to review.
   - If for the time allotment of 210 minutes there are 7 essay questions to answer, that would average about 30 minutes a question. Give yourself only 25 minutes per question so that you have about 35 minutes to review.

6) The most important instruction is to *read each question* and make sure you know what is wanted. The second most important instruction is to *time yourself properly* so that you answer every question. The third most important instruction is to *answer every question*. Guess if you have to but include something for each question. Remember that you will receive no credit for a blank and will probably receive some credit if you write something in answer to an essay question. If you guess a letter – say "B" for a multiple-choice question – you may have guessed right. If you leave a blank as an answer to a multiple-choice question, the examiners may respect your feelings but it will not add a point to your score. Some exams may penalize you for wrong answers, so in such cases *only*, you may not want to guess unless you have some basis for your answer.

7) Suggestions
    a. Objective-type questions
        1. Examine the question booklet for proper sequence of pages and questions
        2. Read all instructions carefully
        3. Skip any question which seems too difficult; return to it after all other questions have been answered
        4. Apportion your time properly; do not spend too much time on any single question or group of questions
        5. Note and underline key words – *all, most, fewest, least, best, worst, same, opposite,* etc.
        6. Pay particular attention to negatives
        7. Note unusual option, e.g., unduly long, short, complex, different or similar in content to the body of the question
        8. Observe the use of "hedging" words – *probably, may, most likely,* etc.
        9. Make sure that your answer is put next to the same number as the question
       10. Do not second-guess unless you have good reason to believe the second answer is definitely more correct
       11. Cross out original answer if you decide another answer is more accurate; do not erase until you are ready to hand your paper in
       12. Answer all questions; guess unless instructed otherwise
       13. Leave time for review

    b. Essay questions
        1. Read each question carefully
        2. Determine exactly what is wanted. Underline key words or phrases.
        3. Decide on outline or paragraph answer
        4. Include many different points and elements unless asked to develop any one or two points or elements
        5. Show impartiality by giving pros and cons unless directed to select one side only
        6. Make and write down any assumptions you find necessary to answer the questions
        7. Watch your English, grammar, punctuation and choice of words
        8. Time your answers; don't crowd material

8) Answering the essay question

Most essay questions can be answered by framing the specific response around several key words or ideas. Here are a few such key words or ideas:

M's: manpower, materials, methods, money, management
P's: purpose, program, policy, plan, procedure, practice, problems, pitfalls, personnel, public relations
    a. Six basic steps in handling problems:
        1. Preliminary plan and background development
        2. Collect information, data and facts
        3. Analyze and interpret information, data and facts
        4. Analyze and develop solutions as well as make recommendations

5. Prepare report and sell recommendations
6. Install recommendations and follow up effectiveness

b. Pitfalls to avoid
1. *Taking things for granted* – A statement of the situation does not necessarily imply that each of the elements is necessarily true; for example, a complaint may be invalid and biased so that all that can be taken for granted is that a complaint has been registered
2. *Considering only one side of a situation* – Wherever possible, indicate several alternatives and then point out the reasons you selected the best one
3. *Failing to indicate follow up* – Whenever your answer indicates action on your part, make certain that you will take proper follow-up action to see how successful your recommendations, procedures or actions turn out to be
4. *Taking too long in answering any single question* – Remember to time your answers properly

EXAMINATION SECTION

VERBAL AND CLERICAL ABILITIES

EXAMINATION SECTION

DIRECTIONS.
Each question or incomplete statement is followed by several suggested answers or completions. Select the one that *BEST* answers the question or completes the statement. *PRINT THE LETTER OF THE CORRECT ANSWER IN THE SPACE AT THE RIGHT.*

Questions 1-5. *Verbal Abilities*

1. BARREN means most nearly
   A. nobleman   B. productive C. bauble   D. empty

1. ...

2. The secretarial profession is a very old one and has increased in importance with the passage of time. In modern times, the vast expansion of business and industry has greatly increased the need and opportunities for secretaries, and for the first time in history their number has become large.
   The statement *BEST* supports the statement that the secretarial profession
   A. is older than business and industry
   B. demands higher training than it did formerly
   C. did not exist in ancient times
   D. has greatly increased in size.

2. ...

Question 3.
DIRECTIONS: In the following question, the first two words in capital letters go together in some way. The third word in capital letters is related in the same way to one of the words lettered A, B, C, or D.

3. ACTOR is to THEATER as MINISTER is to
   A. children   B. people   C. church   D. aisle

3. ...

Question 4.
DIRECTIONS: Find the correct spelling of the word and print the letter of the correct answer in the space at the right. If no suggested spelling is correct, print the letter D.

4.   A. careacteristic   B. characteristic
     C. cheracteristic   D. none of these

4. ...

Question 5.
DIRECTIONS: Decide which sentence is preferable with respect to grammar and usage for a formal letter or report.

5.   A. This booklet is designed to inform teachers about training requirements.
     B. According to the announcement, the new director's interest were many and varied.
     C. He arrived at about noon.
     D. I expect the report is true.

5. ...

Questions 6-8. *Arithmetic*
DIRECTIONS: Work each problem and compare your answers with suggested answers A, B, C, D. If your answer does not agree with any of these suggested answers, print the letter E.

6. Multiply: 26
              x 6
   A. 120   B. 136   C. 146   D. 156
   E. none of these

6. ...

7. Add: 24
         +35

7. ...

    A. 48   B. 49   C. 58   D. 59
    E. none of these

8. Subtract: 27
             - 6

8. ...

    A. 20   B. 21   C. 33   D. 35
    E. none of these

Questions 9-30. *Clerical Aptitude*

Questions 9-13.

DIRECTIONS: Questions 9 through 13 require name and number comparisons. In each line across the page there are three names or numbers that are much alike. Compare the three names or numbers and decide which ones are exactly alike. In the space at the right, print the answer:

    A if *ALL THREE* names or numbers are exactly *ALIKE*
    B if only the *FIRST* and *SECOND* names or numbers are exactly *ALIKE*
    C if only the *FIRST* and *THIRD* names or numbers are exactly *ALIKE*
    D if only the *SECOND* and *THIRD* names or numbers are exactly *ALIKE*
    E if *ALL THREE* names or numbers are *DIFFERENT*

9. Maria Ferster	Maria Fester	Marie Ferster	9. ...
10. Beth Spring	Beth Spring	Beth Springs	
11. Jan Foot	Jan Foote	Jan Foote	
12. 21346	21346	21346	
13. 54836	54386	54836	

Questions 14-16.

DIRECTIONS: There is a name in a box at the left, and four other names in alphabetical order at the right. Find the correct space for the boxed name so that it will be in alphabetical order with the others, and print the letter of that space as your answer.

14. [Penton, Agnes]

    A.
        Pease, Dale   14. ...
    B.
        Penn, David
    C.
        Perdue, Adela
    D.
        Perkins, Gary
    E.

15. [Wallo, Glen]

    A.
        Wallis, Paul   15. ...
    B.
        Walsh, Ralph
    C.
        Walters, Robert
    D.
        Walton, Gail
    E.

16. | Bennett, Paul |
    A.
      Bell, Mae
    B.
      Beman, Marie
    C.
      Bender, Robert
    D.
      Benner, George
    E.

16. ...

Questions 17-20.

DIRECTIONS: In the following questions, do whatever the question says, and find your answer among the list of suggested answers for that question. Mark the sapce at the right A, B, C, or D, for the answer you obtained; or if your answer is not among these, mark E for that question.

17. Add: 23
       +34
    A. 46   B. 47   C. 56   D. 57
    E. none of these

17. ...

18. Subtract: 26
          - 5
    A. 20   B. 21   C. 31   D. 33
    E. none of these

18. ...

19. Multiply: 26
         x 7
    A. 120   B. 146   C. 176   D. 182
    E. none of these

19. ...

20. Divide: 8)168
    A. 20   B. 22   C. 24   D. 26
    E. none of these

20. ...

Questions 21-35.

DIRECTIONS: There is a set of 5 suggested answers for each group of questions that appears below. To find the answer to each question, find which one of the suggested answers contains numbers and letters all of which appear in that question. These numbers and letters may be in any order in the question, but all four must appear. If no suggested answer fits, mark E for that question.

21. 0 Q M 1 I V 6 8   21. ...
22. V 1 9 B 8 N 5 M   22. ...
23. B 9 I M 5 1 0 Q   23. ...
24. 5 M 1 6 8 I B N   24. ...
25. B Q 9 5 0 M V 1   25. ...
    Suggested answers:
      A. 9, 1, I, M   B. 0, 1, V, B
      C. 8, 9, M, B   D. 8, 0, I, V
      E. none of these

26. 1 R N 2 A W 7 9   26. ...
27. W 2 0 C 9 P 6 N   27. ...
28. C O J N 6 2 1 R   28. ...
29. 6 N 2 7 9 J C P   29. ...
30. C R 0 6 1 N W B   30. ...
    Suggested answers:
      A. 0, 2, J, N   B. 1, 2, W, C
      C. 9, 0, N, C   D, 9, 1, J, W
      E. none of these

KEY (CORRECT ANSWERS)

1.	D		16.	E
2.	D		17.	D
3.	C		18.	B
4.	B		19.	D
5.	A		20.	E
6.	D		21.	D
7.	D		22.	C
8.	B		23.	A
9.	E		24.	E
10.	B		25.	B
11.	D		26.	E
12.	A		27.	C
13.	C		28.	A
14.	C		29.	E
15.	B		30.	E

VERBAL ABILITIES TEST

DIRECTIONS AND SAMPLE QUESTIONS

Study the sample questions carefully. Each question has four suggested answers. Decide which one is the best answer. Find the question number on the Sample Answer Sheet. Show your answer to the question by darkening completely the space corresponding to the letter that is the same as the letter of your answer. Keep your mark within the space. If you have to erase a mark, be sure to erase it completely. Mark only one answer for each question. Do NOT mark space E for any question.

SAMPLE VERBAL QUESTIONS

I.   *Previous* means most nearly

   A.   abandoned   C.   timely
   B.   former   D.   younger

II. *(Reading)* "Just as the procedure of a collection department must be clear cut and definite, the steps being taken with the sureness of a skilled chess player, so the various paragraphs of a collection letter must show clear organization, giving evidence of a mind that, from the beginning, has had a specific end in view."
   The quotation best supports the statement that a collection letter should always

   A.   show a spirit of sportsmanship
   B.   be divided into several paragraphs
   C.   be brief, but courteous
   D.   be carefully planned

III. Decide which sentence is preferable with respect to grammar and usage suitable for a formal letter or report.

   A.   They do not ordinarily present these kind of reports in detail like this.
   B.   A report of this kind is not hardly ever given in such detail as this one.
   C.   This report is more detailed than what such reports ordinarily are.
   D.   A report of this kind is not ordinarily presented in as much detail as this one is.

IV. Find the correct spelling of the word and darken the proper answer space. If no suggested spelling is correct, darken space D.

   A.   athalete   C.   athlete
   B.   athelete   D.   none of these

V.   SPEEDOMETER is related to POINTER as WATCH is related to

   A.   case   C.   dial
   B.   hands   D.   numerals

EXAMINATION SECTION
TEST 1

Read each question carefully. Select the best answer and darken the proper space on the answer sheet.

1. *Flexible* means most nearly
   - A. breakable
   - B. flammable
   - C. pliable
   - D. weak

2. *Option* means most nearly
   - A. use
   - B. choice
   - C. value
   - D. blame

3. To *verify* means most nearly to
   - A. examine
   - B. explain
   - C. confirm
   - D. guarantee

4. *Indolent* means most nearly
   - A. moderate
   - B. hopeless
   - C. selfish
   - D. lazy

5. *Respiration* means most nearly
   - A. recovery
   - B. breathing
   - C. pulsation
   - D. sweating

6. PLUMBER is related to WRENCH as PAINTER is related to
   - A. brush
   - B. pipe
   - C. shop
   - D. hammer

7. LETTER is related to MESSAGE as PACKAGE is related to
   - A. sender
   - B. merchandise
   - C. insurance
   - D. business

8. FOOD is related to HUNGER as SLEEP is related to
   - A. night
   - B. dream
   - C. weariness
   - D. rest

9. KEY is related to TYPEWRITER as DIAL is related to
   - A. sun
   - B. number
   - C. circle
   - D. telephone

Grammar

10.
   - A. I think that they will promote whoever has the best record.
   - B. The firm would have liked to have promoted all employees with good records.
   - C. Such of them that have the best records have excellent prospects of promotion.
   - D. I feel sure they will give the promotion to whomever has the best record.

11. A. The receptionist must answer courteously the questions of all them callers.
    B. The receptionist must answer courteously the questions what are asked by the callers.
    C. There would have been no trouble if the receptionist had have always answered courteously.
    D. The receptionist should answer courteously the questions of all callers.

Spelling

12. A. collapsible
    B. collapseble
    C. collapseble
    D. none of these

13. A. ambigeuous
    B. ambigeous
    C. ambiguous
    D. none of these

14. A. predesessor
    B. predecesar
    C. predecesser
    D. none of these

15. A. sanctioned
    B. sancktioned
    C. sanctionned
    D. none of these

Reading

16. "The secretarial profession is a very old one and has increased in importance with the passage of time. In modern times, the vast expansion of business and industry has greatly increased the need and opportunities for secretaries, and for the first time in history their number has become large."
    The quotation best supports the statement that the secretarial profession

    A. is older than business and industry
    B. did not exist in ancient times
    C. has greatly increased in size
    D. demands higher training than it did formerly

17. "Civilization started to move ahead more rapidly when man freed himself of the shackles that restricted his search for the truth."
    The quotation best supports the statement that the progress of civilization

    A. came as a result of man's dislike for obstacles
    B. did not begin until restrictions on learning were removed
    C. has been aided by man's efforts to find
    D. the truth is based on continually increasing efforts

18. *Vigilant* means most nearly

    A. sensible
    B. watchful
    C. suspicious
    D. restless

19. *Incidental* means most nearly

    A. independent
    B. needless
    C. infrequent
    D. casual

7

20. *Conciliatory* means most nearly

    A. pacific
    B. contentious
    C. obligatory
    D. offensive

21. *Altercation* means most nearly

    A. defeat
    B. concurrence
    C. controversy
    D. vexation

22. *Irresolute* means most nearly

    A. wavering
    B. insubordinate
    C. impudent
    D. unobservant

23. DARKNESS is related to SUNLIGHT as STILLNESS is related to

    A. quiet
    B. moonlight
    C. sound
    D. dark

24. DESIGNED is related to INTENTION as ACCIDENTAL is related to

    A. purpose
    B. caution
    C. damage
    D. chance

25. ERROR is related to PRACTICE as SOUND is related to

    A. deafness
    B. noise
    C. muffler
    D. horn

26. RESEARCH is related to FINDINGS as TRAINING is related to

    A. skill
    B. tests
    C. supervision
    D. teaching

27. A If properly addressed, the letter will reach my mother and I.
    B. The letter had been addressed to myself and my mother,
    C. I believe the letter was addressed to either my mother or I.
    D. My mother's name, as well as mine, was on the letter.

28. A. The supervisor reprimanded the typist, whom she believed had made careless errors.
    B. The typist would have corrected the errors had she of known that the supervisor would see the report.
    C. The errors in the typed report were so numerous that they could hardly beoverlooked.
    D. Many errors were found in the report which she typed and could not disregard them.

29. A. minieture
    B. minneature
    C. mineature
    D. none of these

30. A. extemporaneous
    B. extempuraneus
    C. extemporaneous
    D. none of these

31. A. problemmatical
    B. problematical
    C. problematicle
    D. none of these

32. A. descendant
     B. decendant
     C. desendant
     D. none of these

33. "The likelihood of America's exhausting her natural resources seems to be growing less. All kinds of waste are being reworked and new uses are constantly being found for almost everything. We are getting more use out of our goods and are making many new byproducts out of what was formerly thrown away."
     The quotation best supports the statement that we seem to be in less danger of exhausting our resources because

     A. economy is found to lie in the use of substitutes
     B. more service is obtained from a given amount of material
     C. we are allowing time for nature to restore them
     D. supply and demand are better controlled

34. "Memos should be clear, concise, and brief. Omit all unnecessary words. The parts of speech most often used in memos are nouns, verbs, adjectives, and adverbs. If possible, do without pronouns, prepositions, articles and copulative verbs. Use simple sentences, rather than complex or compound ones."
     The quotation best supports the statement that in writing memos one should always use

     A. common and simple words
     B. only nouns, verbs, adjectives, and adverbs
     C. incomplete sentences
     D. only the words essential to the meaning.

35. To *counteract* means most nearly to

     A. undermine
     B. censure
     C. preserve
     D. neutralize

36. *Deferred* means most nearly

     A. reversed
     B. delayed
     C. considered
     D. forbidden

37. *Feasible* means most nearly

     A. capable
     B. justifiable
     C. practicable
     D. beneficial

38. To *encounter* means most nearly to

     A. meet
     B. recall
     C. overcome
     D. retreat

39. *Innate* means most nearly

     A. eternal
     B. well-developed
     C. native
     D. prospective

40. STUDENT is related to TEACHER as DISCIPLE is related to

     A. follower
     B. master
     C. principal
     D. pupil

9

41. LECTURE is related to AUDITORIUM as EXPERIMENT is related to

    A. scientist
    B. chemistry
    C. laboratory
    D. discovery

42. BODY is related to FOOD as ENGINE is related to

    A. wheels
    B. fuel
    C. motion
    D. smoke

43. SCHOOL is related to EDUCATION as THEATER is related to

    A. management
    B. stage
    C. recreation
    D. preparation

44.   A. Most all these statements have been supported by persons who are reliable and can be depended upon.
    B. The persons which have guaranteed these statements are reliable.
    C. Reliable persons guarantee the facts with regards to the truth of these statements.
    D. These statements can be depended on, for their truth has been guaranteed by reliable persons.

45.   A. The success of the book pleased both his publisher and he.
    B. Both his publisher and he was pleased with the success of the book.
    C. Neither he or his publisher was disappointed with the success of the book.
    D. His publisher was as pleased as he with the success of the book

46.   A. extercate
    B. extracate
    C. extricate
    D. none of these

47.   A. hereditory
    B. hereditary
    C. hereditairy
    D. none of these

48.   A. auspiceous
    B. auspiseous
    C. auspicious
    D. none of these

49.   A. sequance
    B. sequence
    C. sequense
    D. none of these

50. "The prevention of accidents makes it necessary not only that safety devices be used to guard exposed machinery but also that mechanics be instructed in safety rules which they must follow for their own protection, and that the lighting in the plant be adequate."
The quotation best supports the statement that industrial accidents

    A. may be due to ignorance
    B. are always avoidable
    C. usually result from inadequate machinery
    D. cannot be entirely overcome

51. "The English language is peculiarly rich in synonyms, and there is scarcely a language spoken among men that has not some representative in English speech. The spirit of the Anglo-Saxon race has subjugated these various elements to one idiom, making not a patchwork, but a composite language."
The quotation best supports the statement that the English language

A. has few idiomatic expressions
B. is difficult to translate
C. is used universally
D. has absorbed words from other languages

52. To *acquiesce* means most nearly to

    A. assent
    B. acquire
    C. complete
    D. participate

53. *Unanimity* means most nearly

    A. emphasis
    B. namelessness
    C. harmony
    D. impartiality

54. *Precedent* means most nearly

    A. example
    B. theory
    C. law
    D. conformity

55. *Versatile* means most nearly

    A. broad-minded
    B. well-known
    C. up-to-date
    D. many-sided

56. *Authentic* means most nearly

    A. detailed
    B. reliable
    C. valuable
    D. practical

57. BIOGRAPHY is related to FACT as NOVEL is related to

    A. fiction
    B. literature
    C. narration
    D. book

58. COPY is related to CARBON PAPER as MOTION PICTURE is related to

    A. theater
    B. film
    C. duplicate
    D. television

59. EFFICIENCY is related to REWARD as CARELESSNESS is related to

    A. improvement
    B. disobedience
    C. reprimand
    D. repetition

60. ABUNDANT is related to CHEAP as SCARCE is related to

    A. ample
    B. costly
    C. inexpensive
    D. unobtainable

61. A   Brown's & Company employees have recently received increases in salary.
    B.   Brown & Company recently increased the salaries of all its employees.
    C.   Recently, Brown & Company has increased their employees' salaries.
    D.   Brown & Company have recently increased the salaries of all its employees

62. A. In reviewing the typists' work reports, the job analyst found records of unusual typing speeds.
     B. It says in the job analyst's report that some employees type with great speed.
     C. The job analyst found that, in reviewing the typists' work reports, that some unusual typing speeds had been made.
     D. In the reports of typists' speeds, the job analyst found some records that are kind of unusual.

63. A. obliterate
     B. oblitterat
     C. obbliterate
     D. none of these

64. A. diagnoesis
     B. diagnossis
     C. diagnosis
     D. none of these

65. A. contenance
     B. countenance
     C. knowledge
     D. none of these

66. A. conceivably
     B. concieveably
     C. conceiveably
     D. none of these

67. "Through advertising, manufacturers exercise a high degree of control over consumers' desires. However, the manufacturer assumes enormous risks in attempting to predict what consumers will want and in producing goods in quantity and distributing them in advance of final selection by the consumers."
     The quotation best supports the statement that manufacturers

     A. can eliminate the risk of overproduction by advertising
     B. distribute goods directly to the consumers
     C. must depend upon the final consumers for the success of their undertakings
     D. can predict with great accuracy the success of any product they put on the market

68. "In the relations of man to nature, the procuring of food and shelter is fundamental. With the migration of man to various climates, ever new adjustments to the food supply and to the climate became necessary."
     The quotation best supports the statement that the means by which man supplies his material needs are

     A. accidental
     B. varied
     C. limited
     D. inadequate

69. *Strident* means most nearly

     A. swaggering
     B. domineering
     C. angry
     D. harsh

70. To *confine* means most nearly to

     A. hide
     B. restrict
     C. eliminate
     D. punish

71. To *accentuate* means most nearly to

     A. modify
     B. hasten
     C. sustain
     D. intensify

12

72. *Banal* means most nearly

   A. commonplace
   B. forceful
   C. tranquil
   D. indifferent

73. *Incorrigible* means most nearly

   A. intolerable
   B. retarded
   C. irreformable
   D. brazen

74. POLICEMAN is related to ORDER as DOCTOR is related to

   A. physician
   B. hospital
   C. sickness
   D. health

75. ARTIST is related to EASEL as WEAVER is related to

   A. loom
   B. cloth
   C. threads
   D. spinner

76. CROWD is related to PERSONS as FLEET is related to

   A. expedition
   B. officers
   C. navy
   D. ships

77. CALENDAR is related to DATE as MAP is related to

   A. geography
   B. trip
   C. mileage
   D. vacation

78. A Since the report lacked the needed information, it was of no use to him.
     B. This report was useless to him because there were no needed information in it.
     C. Since the report did not contain the needed information, it was not real useful to him.
     D. Being that the report lacked the needed information, he could not use it.

79. A The company had hardly declared the dividend till the notices were prepared for mailing.
     B. They had no sooner declared the dividend when they sent the notices to the stockholders.
     C. No sooner had the dividend been declared than the notices were prepared for mailing.
     D. Scarcely had the dividend been declared than the notices were sent out.

80. A. compitition
     B. competition
     C. competetion
     D. none of these

81. A. occassion
     B. occasion
     C. ocassion
     D. none of these

82. A. knowlege
     B. knolledge
     C. knowledge
     D. none of these

83. A. deliborate
     B. deliberate
     C. delibrate
     D. none of these

13

84. "What constitutes skill in any line of work is not always easy to determine; economy of time must be carefully distinguished from economy of energy, as the quickest method may require the greatest expenditure of muscular effort, and may not be essential or at all desirable."

The quotation best supports the statement that

   A.   the most efficiently executed task is not always the one done in the shortest time
   B.   energy and time cannot both be conserved in performing a single task
   C.   a task is well done when it is performed in the shortest time
   D.   skill in performing a task should not be acquired at the expense of time

85. "It is difficult to distinguish between bookkeeping and accounting. In attempts to do so, bookkeeping is called the art, and accounting the science, of recording business transactions. Bookkeeping gives the history of the business in a systematic manner; and accounting classifies, analyzes, and interprets the facts thus recorded."

The quotation best supports the statement that

   A.   accounting is less systematic than bookkeeping
   B.   accounting and bookkeeping are closely related
   C.   bookkeeping and accounting cannot be distinguished from one another
   D.   bookkeeping has been superseded by accounting

———

KEY (CORRECT ANSWERS)

1. C	21. C	41. C	61. B	81. B
2. B	22. A	42. B	62. A	82. C
3. C	23. C	43. C	63. A	83. B
4. D	24. D	44. D	64. C	84. A
5. B	25. C	45. D	65. B	85. B
6. A	26. A	46. C	66. A	
7. B	27. D	47. B	67. C	
8. C	28. C	48. C	68. B	
9. D	29. D	49. B	69. D	
10. A	30. A	50. A	70. B	
11. D	31. B	51. D	71. D	
12. A	32. A	52. A	72. A	
13. C	33. B	53. C	73. C	
14. D	34. D	54. A	74. D	
15. A	35. D	55. D	75. A	
16. C	36. B	56. B	76. D	
17. C	37. C	57. A	77. C	
18. B	38. A	58. B	78. A	
19. D	39. C	59. C	79. C	
20. A	40. B	60. B	80. B	

TEST 2

Read each question carefully. Select the best answer and blacken the proper space on the answer sheet.

1. *Option* means most nearly

    A. use
    B. choice
    C. value
    D. blame
    E. mistake

2. *Irresolute* means most nearly

    A. wavering
    B. insubordinate
    C. impudent
    D. determined
    E. unobservant

3. *Flexible* means most nearly

    A. breakable
    B. inflammable
    C. pliable
    D. weak
    E. impervious

4. To *counteract* means most nearly to

    A. undermine
    B. censure
    C. preserve
    D. sustain
    E. neutralize

5. To *verify* means most nearly to

    A. justify
    B. explain
    C. confirm
    D. guarantee
    E. examine

6. *Indolent* means most nearly

    A. moderate
    B. relentless
    C. selfish
    D. lazy
    E. hopeless

7. To say that an action is *deferred* means most nearly that it is

    A. delayed
    B. reversed
    C. considered
    D. forbidden
    E. followed

8. To *encounter* means most nearly to

    A. meet
    B. recall
    C. overcome
    D. weaken
    E. retreat

9. *Feasible* means most nearly

    A. capable
    B. practicable
    C. justifiable
    D. beneficial
    E. reliable

10. *Respiration* means most nearly

    A. dehydration   D. sweating
    B. breathing   E. recovery
    C. pulsation

11. *Vigilant* means most nearly

    A. sensible   D. suspicious
    B. ambitious   E. restless
    C. watchful

12. To say that an action is taken *before the proper time* means most nearly that it is taken

    A. prematurely   D. punctually
    B. furtively   E. presently
    C. temporarily

13. *Innate* means most nearly

    A. eternal   D. prospective
    B. learned   E. well-developed
    C. native

14. *Precedent* means most nearly

    A. duplicate   D. conformity
    B. theory   E. example
    C. law

15. To say that the flow of work into an office is *incessant* means most nearly that it is

    A. more than can be handled
    B. uninterrupted
    C. scanty
    D. decreasing in volume
    E. orderly

16. *Unanimity* means most nearly

    A. emphasis   D. harmony
    B. namelessness   E. impartiality
    C. disagreement

17. *Incidental* means most nearly

    A. independent   D. necessary
    B. needless   E. casual
    C. infrequent

18. *Versatile* means most nearly

    A. broad-minded   D. many-sided
    B. well-Known   E. up-to-date
    C. old-fashioned

19. *Conciliatory* means most nearly

A. pacific
B. contentious
C. disorderly

D. obligatory
E. offensive

20. *Altercation* means most nearly

A. defeat
B. concurrence
C. controversy

D. consensus
E. vexation

21. *(Reading)* "The secretarial profession is a very old one and has increased in importance with the passage of time. In modern times, the vast expansion of business and industry has greatly increased the need and opportunities for secretaries, and for the first time in history their number has become large."

The quotation best supports the statement that the secretarial profession

A. is older than business and industry
B. did not exist in ancient times
C. has greatly increased in size
D. demands higher training than it did formerly
E. has always had many members

22. *(Reading)* "The modern system of production unites various kinds of workers into a well-organized body in which each has a definite place."
The quotation best supports the statement that the modern system of production

A. increases production
B. trains workers
C. simplifies tasks
D. combines and places workers
E. combines the various plants

23. *(Reading)* "The prevention of accidents makes it necessary not only that safety devices be used to guard exposed machinery but also that mechanics be instructed in safety rules which they must follow for their own protection, and that the lighting in the plant be adequate."

The quotation best supports the statement that industrial accidents

A. may be due to ignorance
B. are always avoidable
C. usually result from inadequate machinery
D. cannot be entirely overcome
E. result in damage to machinery

24. *(Reading)* "It is wise to choose a duplicating machine that will do the work required with the greatest efficiency and at the least cost. Users with a large volume of business need speedy machines that cost little to operate and are well made."

The quotation best supports the statement that

A. most users of duplicating machines prefer low operating cost to efficiency
B. a well-built machine will outlast a cheap one
C. a duplicating machine is not efficient unless it is sturdy
D. a duplicating machine should be both efficient and economical
E. in duplicating machines speed is more usual than low operating cost

25. *(Reading)* "The likelihood of America's exhausting her natural resources seems to be growing less. All kinds of waste are being reworked and new uses are constantly being found for almost everything. We are getting more use out of our goods and are making many new byproducts out of what was formerly thrown away."

The quotation best supports the statement that we seem to be in less danger of exhausting our resources because

A. economy is found to lie in the use of substitutes
B. more service is obtained from a given amount of material
C. more raw materials are being produced
D. supply and demand are better controlled
E. we are allowing time for nature to restore them

26. *(Reading)* "Probably few people realize, as they drive on a concrete road, that steel is used to keep the surface flat and even, in spite of the weight of busses and trucks. Steel bars, deeply imbedded in the concrete, provide sinews to take the stresses so that they cannot crack the slab or make it wavy."

The quotation best supports the statement that a concrete road

A. is expensive to build
B. usually cracks under heavy weights
C. looks like any other road
D. is used exclusively for heavy traffic
E. is reinforced with other material

27. *(Reading)* "Through advertising, manufacturers exercise a high degree of control over consumers' desires. However, the manufac-turer assumes enormous risks in attempting to predict what consumers will want and in producing goods in quantity and distributing them in advance of final selection by the consumers."

The quotation best supports the statement that manufacturers

A. can eliminate the risk of overproduction by advertising
B. completely control buyers' needs and desires
C. must depend upon the final consumers for the success of their undertakings
D. distribute goods directly to the consumers
E. can predict with great accuracy the success of any product they put on the market

28. *(Reading)* "Success in shorthand, like success in any other study, depends upon the interest the student takes in it. In writing shorthand it is not sufficient to know how to write a word correctly; one must also be able to write it quickly."

The quotation best supports the statement that

    A.   one must be able to read shorthand as well as to write it
    B.   shorthand requires much study
    C.   if a student can write correctly, he can also write quickly
    D.   proficiency in shorthand requires both speed and accuracy
    E.   interest in shorthand makes study unnecessary

29.   *(Reading)* "The countries in the Western Hemisphere were settled by people who were ready each day for new adventure. The peoples of North and South America have retained, in addition to expectant and forwardlooking attitudes, the ability and the willingness that they have often shown in the past to adapt themselves to new conditions."

    The quotation best supports the statement that the peoples in the Western Hemisphere

    A.   no longer have fresh adventures daily
    B.   are capable of making changes as new situations arise
    C.   are no more forward-looking than the peoples of other regions
    D.   tend to resist regulations
    E.   differ considerably among themselves

30.   *(Reading)* "Civilization started to move ahead more rapidly when man freed himself of the shackles that restricted his search for the truth."
    The quotation best supports the statement that the progress of civilization

    A.   came as a result of man's dislike for obstacles
    B.   did not begin until restrictions on learning were removed
    C.   has been aided by man's efforts to find the truth
    D.   is based on continually increasing efforts
    E.   continues at a constantly increasing rate

31.   *(Reading)* "It is difficult to distinguish between bookkeeping and accounting. In attempts to do so, bookkeeping is called the art, and accounting the science, of recording business transactions. Bookkeeping gives the history of the business in a systematic manner, and accounting classifies, analyzes, and interprets the facts thus recorded."

    The quotation best supports the statement that

    A.   accounting is less systematic than bookkeeping
    B.   accounting and bookkeeping are closely related
    C.   bookkeeping and accounting cannot be distinguished from one another
    D.   bookkeeping has been superseded by accounting
    E.   the facts recorded by bookkeeping may be interpreted in many ways

32.   *(Reading)* "Some specialists are willing to give their services to the Government entirely free of charge; some feel that a nominal salary, such as will cover traveling expenses, is sufficient for a position that is recognized as being somewhat honorary in nature; many other specialists value their time so highly that they will not devote any of it to public service that does not repay them at a rate commensurate with the fees that they can obtain from a good private clientele."

    The quotation best supports the statement that the use of specialists by the Government

A. is rare because of the high cost of securing such persons
B. may be influenced by the willingness of specialists to serve
C. enables them to secure higher salaries in private fields
D. has become increasingly common during the past few years
E. always conflicts with private demands for their services

33. *(Reading)* "The leader of an industrial enterprise has two principal functions. He must manufacture and distribute a product at a profit, and he must keep individuals and groups of individuals working effectively together."

    The quotation best supports the statement that an industrial leader should be able to

    A. increase the distribution of his plant's product
    B. introduce large-scale production methods
    C. coordinate the activities of his employees
    D. profit by the experience of other leaders
    E. expand the business rapidly

34. *(Reading)* "The coloration of textile fabrics composed of cotton and wool generally requires two processes, as the process used in dyeing wool is seldom capable of fixing the color upon cotton. The usual method is to immerse the fabric in the requisite baths to dye the wool and then to treat the partially dyed material in the manner found suitable for cotton."
    The quotation best supports the statement that the dyeing of textile fabrics composed of cotton and wool

    A. is less complicated than the dyeing of wool alone
    B. is more successful when the material contains more cotton than wool
    C. is not satisfactory when solid colors are desired
    D. is restricted to two colors for any one fabric
    E. is usually based upon the methods required for dyeing the different materials

35. *(Reading)* "The fact must not be overlooked that only about one-half of the international trade of the world crosses the oceans. The other half is merely exchanges of merchandise between countries lying alongside each other or at least within the same continent."

    The quotation best supports the statement that

    A. the most important part of any country's trade is transoceanic
    B. domestic trade is insignificant when compared with foreign trade
    C. the exchange of goods between neighboring countries is not considered international trade
    D. foreign commerce is not necessarily carried on by water
    E. about one-half of the trade of the world is international

36. *(Reading)* "In the relations of man to nature, the procuring of food and shelter is fundamental. With the migration of man to various climates, ever new adjustments to the food supply and to the climate became necessary."

    The quotation best supports the statement that the means by which man supplies his material needs are

A. accidental
B. varied
C. limited

D. uniform
E. inadequate

37. *(Reading)* "Every language has its peculiar word associations that have no basis in logic and cannot therefore be reasoned about. These idiomatic expressions are ordinarily acquired only by much reading and conversation although questions about such matters may sometimes be answered by the dictionary. Dictionaries large enough to include quota-tions from standard authors are especially serviceable in determining questions of idiom."

The quotation best supports the statement that idiomatic expressions

A. give rise to meaningless arguments because they have no logical basis
B. are widely used by recognized authors.
C. are explained in most dictionaries
D. are more common in some languages than in others
E. are best learned by observation of the language as actually used

38. *(Reading)* "Individual differences in mental traits assume importance in fitting workers to jobs because such personal characteristics are persistent and are relatively little influenced by training and experience."

The quotation best supports the statement that training and experience

A. are limited in their effectiveness in fitting workers to jobs
B. do not increase a worker's fitness for a job
C. have no effect upon a person's mental traits
D. have relatively little effect upon the individual's chances for success
E. should be based on the mental traits of an individual

39. *(Reading)* "The telegraph networks of the country now constitute wonderfully operated institutions, affording for ordinary use of modern, business an important means of communication. The transmission of messages by electricity has reached the goal for which the postal service has long been striving, namely, the elimination of distance as an effective barrier of communication."

The quotation best supports the statement that

A. a new standard of communication has been attained
B. in the telegraph service, messages seldom go astray
C. it is the distance between the parties which creates the need for communication
D. modern business relies more upon the telegraph than upon the mails
E. the telegraph is a form of postal service

40. *(Reading)* "The competition of buyers tends to keep prices up, the competition of sellers to send them down. Normally the pressure of competition among sellers is stronger than that among buyers since the seller has his article to sell and must get rid of it, whereas the buyer is not committed to anything."

The quotation best supports the statement that low prices are caused by

A. buyer competition
B. competition of buyers with sellers fluctuations in demand
C. greater competition among sellers than among buyers
D. more sellers than buyers

In each question from 41 through 60, find the CORRECT spelling of the word, and blacken the proper space on your answer sheet. Sometimes there is no correct spelling; if none of the suggested spellings is correct, blacken space D on your answer sheet.

41. A. compitition   C. competetion
     B. competition   D. none of these

42. A. diagnoesis   C. diagnosis
     B. diagnossis   D. none of these

43. A. contenance   C. countinance
     B. countenance   D. none of these

44. A. deliborate   C. delibrate
     B. deliberate   D. none of these

45. A. knowlege   C. knowledge
     B. knolledge   D. none of these

46. A. occassion   C. ocassion
     B. occasion   D. none of these

47. A. sanctioned   C. sanctionned
     B. sancktioned   D. none of these

48. A. predesessor   C. predecesser
     B. predecesar   D. none of these

49. A. problemmatical   C. problematicle
     B. problematical   D. none of these

50. A. descendant   C. desendant
     B. decendant   D. none of these

51. A. collapsible   C. collapseble
     B. collapseable   D. none of these

52. A. sequance   C. sequense
     B. sequence   D. none of these

53. A. oblitorate   C. obbliterate
     B. oblitterat   D. none of these

54. A. ambigeuous   C. ambiguous
     B. ambigeous   D. none of these

55. A. minieture   C. mineature
     B. minneature   D. none of these

56. A. extemporaneous   C. extemperaneous
     B. extempuraneus   D. none of these

57. A. hereditory   C. hereditairy
     B. hereditary   D. none of these

58. A. conceivably   C. conceiveably
     B. concieveably   D. none of these

59. A. extercate   C. extricate
     B. extracate   D. none of these

60. A. auspiceous   C. auspicious
     B. auspiseous   D. none of these

Select the sentence that is preferable with respect to grammar and usage such as would be suitable in a formal letter or report. Then blacken the proper space on the answer sheet.

61. A The receptionist must answer courteously the questions of all them callers.
     B. The questions of all callers had ought to be answered courteously.
     C. The receptionist must answer courteously the questions what are asked by the callers.
     D. There would have been no trouble if the receptionist had have always answered courteously.
     E. The receptionist should answer courteously the questions of all callers.

62. A I had to learn a great number of rules, causing me to dislike the course.
     B. I disliked that study because it required the learning of numerous rules.
     C. I disliked that course very much, caused by the numerous rules I had to memorize.
     D. The cause of my dislike was on account of the numerous rules I had to learn in that course.
     E. The reason I disliked this study was because there were numerous rules that had to be learned.

63. A If properly addressed, the letter will reach my mother and I.
     B. The letter had been addressed to myself and mother.
     C. I believe the letter was addressed to either my mother or I.
     D. My mother's name, as well as mine, was on the letter.
     E. If properly addressed, the letter it will reach either my mother or me.

64. A A knowledge of commercial subjects and a mastery of English are essential if one wishes to be a good secretary. ·
     B. Two things necessary to a good secretary are that she should speak good English and to know commercial subjects.
     C. One cannot be a good secretary without she knows commercial subjects and English grammar.
     D. Having had good training in commercial subjects, the rules of English grammar should also be followed.
     E. A secretary seldom or ever succeeds without training in English as well as in commercial subjects.

65. A He suspicions that the service is not so satisfactory as it should be.
    B. He believes that we should try and find whether the service is satisfactory.
    C. He raises the objection that the way which the service is given is not satisfactory.
    D. He believes that the quality of our services are poor.
    E. He believes that the service that we are giving is unsatisfactory.

66. A Most all these statements have been supported by persons who are reliable and can be depended upon.
    B. The persons which have guaranteed these statements are reliable.
    C. Reliable persons guarantee the facts with regards to the truth of these statements.
    D. These statements can be depended on, for their truth has been guaranteed by reliable persons.
    E. Persons as reliable as what these are can be depended upon to make accurate statements.

67. A Brown's & Company's employees have all been given increases in salary.
    B. Brown & Company recently increased the salaries of all its employees.
    C. Recently Brown & Company has in-creased their employees' salaries.
    D. Brown's & Company employees have recently received increases in salary.
    E. Brown & Company have recently increased the salaries of all its employees.

68. A. The personnel office has charge of employment, dismissals, and employee's welfare.
    B. Employment, together with dismissals and employees' welfare, are handled by the personnel department.
    C. The personnel office takes charge of employment, dismissals, and etc.
    D. The personnel office hires and dismisses employees, and their welfare is also its responsibility.
    E. The personnel office is responsible for the employment, dismissal, and welfare of employees.

69. A. This kind of pen is some better than that kind.
    B. I prefer having these pens than any other.
    C. This kind of pen is the most satisfactory for my use.
    D. In comparison with that kind of pen, this kind is more preferable.
    E. If I were to select between them all, I should pick this pen.

70. A. He could not make use of the report, as it was lacking of the needed information.
    B. This report was useless to him because there were no needed information in it.
    C. Since the report lacked the needed information, it was of no use to him.
    D. Being that the report lacked the needed information, he could not use it.
    E. Since the report did not contain the needed information, it was not real useful to him.

71. A. The paper we use for this purpose must be light, glossy, and stand hard usage as well.
    B. Only a light and a glossy, but durable, paper must be used for this purpose.
    C. For this purpose, we want a paper that is light, glossy, but that will stand hard wear.
    D. For this purpose, paper that is light, glossy, and durable is essential.
    E. Light and glossy paper, as well as standing hard usage, is necessary for this purpose.

72. A The company had hardly declared the dividend till the notices were prepared for mailing.
     B. They had no sooner declared the dividend when they sent the notices to the stockholders.
     C. No sooner had the dividend been declared than the notices were prepared for mailing.
     D. Scarcely had the dividend been declared than the notices were sent out.
     E. The dividend had not scarcely been declared when the notices were ready for mailing.

73. A Of all the employees, he spends the most time at the office.
     B. He spends more time at the office than that of his employees.
     C. His working hours are longer or at least equal to those of the other employees.
     D. He devotes as much, if not more, time to his work than the rest of the employees.
     E. He works the longest of any other employee in the office.

74. A In the reports of typists' speeds, the job analyst found some records that are kind of unusual.
     B. It says in the job analyst's report that some employees type with great speed.
     C. The job analyst found that, in reviewing the typists' work Reports, that some unusual typing speeds had been made.
     D. Work reports showing typing speeds include some typists who are unusual.
     E. In reviewing the typists' work reports, the job analyst found records of unusual typing speeds.

75. A It is quite possible that we shall reemploy anyone whose training fits them to do the work.
     B. It is probable that we shall reemploy those who have been trained to do the work.
     C. Such of our personnel that have been trained to do the work will be again employed.
     D. We expect to reemploy the ones who have had training enough that they can do the work.
     E. Some of these people have been trained

76. A He as well as his publisher were pleased with the success of the book.
     B. The success of the book pleased both his publisher and he.
     C. Both his publisher and he was pleased with the success of the book.
     D. Neither he or his publisher was disappointed with the success of the book.
     E. His publisher was as pleased as he with the success of the book.

77. A You have got to get rid of some of these people if you expect to have the quality of the work improve.
     B. The quality of the work would improve if they would leave fewer people do it.
     C. I believe it would be desirable to have fewer persons doing this work.
     D. If you had planned on employing fewer people than this to do the work, this situation would not have arose.
     E. Seeing how you have all those people on that work, it is not surprising that you have a great deal of confusion.

78. A She made lots of errors in her typed report, and which caused her to be repri-
        manded.
     B. The supervisor reprimanded the typist, whom she believed had made careless
        errors.
     C. Many errors were found in the report which she typed and could not disregard
        them.
     D. The typist would have corrected the errors, had she of known that the super-
        visor would see the report.
     E. The errors in the typed report were so numerous that they could hardly be over-
        looked.

79. A. This kind of a worker achieves success through patience.
     B. Success does not often come to men of this type except they who are patient.
     C. Because they are patient, these sort of workers usually achieve success.
     D. This worker has more patience than any man in his office.
     E. This kind of worker achieves success through patience.

80. A. I think that they will promote whoever has the best record.
     B. The firm would have liked to have promoted all employees with good records.
     C. Such of them that have the best records have excellent prospects of promotion.
     D. I feel sure they will give the promotion to whomever has the best record.
     E. Whoever they find to have the best record will, I think, be promoted.

KEY (CORRECT ANSWERS)

1. B	21. C	41. B	61. E
2. A	22. D	42. C	62. B
3. C	23. A	43. B	63. D
4. E	24. D	44. B	64. A
5. C	25. B	45. C	65. E
6. D	26. E	46. B	66. D
7. A	27. C	47. A	67. B
8. A	28. D	48. D	68. E
9. B	29. B	49. B	69. C
10. B	30. C	50. A	70. C
11. C	31. B	51. A	71. D
12. A	32. B	52. B	72. C
13. C	33. C	53. D	73. A
14. E	34. E	54. C	74. E
15. B	35. D	55. D	75. B
16. D	36. B	56. A	76. E
17. E	37. E	57. B	77. C
18. D	38. A	58. A	78. E
19. A	39. A	59. C	79. E
20. C	40. D	60. C	80. A

EXAMINATION SECTION
TEST 1

DIRECTIONS: Each question or incomplete statement is followed by several suggested answers or completions. Select the one that BEST answers the question or completes the statement. *PRINT THE LETTER OF THE CORRECT ANSWER IN THE SPACE AT THE RIGHT.*

Questions 1-10.

WORD MEANING

DIRECTIONS: Each question from 1 to 10 contains a word in capitals followed by four suggested meanings of the word. For each question, choose the best meaning. *PRINT THE LETTER OF THE CORRECT ANSWER IN THE SPACE AT THE RIGHT.*

1. ACCURATE   1.____
    A. correct   B. useful   C. afraid   D. careless

2. ALTER   2.____
    A. copy   B. change   C. report   D. agree

3. DOCUMENT   3.____
    A. outline   B. agreement   C. blueprint   D. record

4. INDICATE   4.____
    A. listen   B. show   C. guess   D. try

5. INVENTORY   5.____
    A. custom   B. discovery   C. warning   D. list

6. ISSUE   6.____
    A. annoy   B. use up   C. give out   D. gain

7. NOTIFY   7.____
    A. inform   B. promise   C. approve   D. strengthen

8. ROUTINE   8.____
    A. path   B. mistake   C. habit   D. journey

9. TERMINATE   9.____
    A. rest   B. start   C. deny   D. end

10. TRANSMIT   10.____
    A. put in   B. send   C. stop   D. go across

Questions 11-15.

READING COMPREHENSION

DIRECTIONS: Questions 11 through 15 test how well you understand what you read. It will be necessary for you to read carefully because your answers to these questions should be based ONLY on the information given in the following paragraphs.

The recipient gains an impression of a typewritten letter before he begins to read the message. Pastors which provide for a good first impression include margins and spacing that are visually pleasing, formal parts of the letter which are correctly placed according to the style of the letter, copy which is free of obvious erasures and over-strikes, and transcript that is even and clear. The problem for the typist is that of how to produce that first, positive impression of her work.

There are several general rules which a typist can follow when she wishes to prepare a properly spaced letter on a sheet of letter-head. Ordinarily, the width of a letter should not be less than four inches nor more than six inches. The side margins should also have a desirable relation to the bottom margin and the space between the letterhead and the body of the letter. Usually the most appealing arrangement is when the side margins are even and the bottom margin is slightly wider than the side margins. In some offices, however, standard line length is used for all business letters, and the secretary then varies the spacing between the date line and the inside address according to the length of the letter.

11.   The BEST title for the above paragraphs would be: 11.___

    A.   Writing Office Letters
    B.   Making Good First Impressions
    C.   Judging Well-Typed Letters
    D.   Good Placing and Spacing for Office Letters

12.   According to the above paragraphs, which of the following might be considered the way   12.___
    in which people very quickly judge the quality of work which has been typed? By

    A.   measuring the margins to see if they are correct
    B.   looking at the spacing and cleanliness of the typescript
    C.   scanning the body of the letter for meaning
    D.   reading the date line and address for errors

13.   What, according to the above paragraphs, would be definitely UNDESIRABLE as the   13.___
    average line length of a typed letter?

    A.   4"   B.   5"   C.   6"   D.   7"

14.   According to the above paragraphs, when the line length is kept standard, the secretary   14.___

    A.   does not have to vary the spacing at all since this also is standard
    B.   adjusts the spacing between the date line and inside address for different lengths of letters
    C.   uses the longest line as a guideline for spacing between the date line and inside address
    D.   varies the number of spaces between the lines

15. According to the above paragraphs, side margins are MOST pleasing when they   15.____

    A.   are even and somewhat smaller than the bottom margin
    B.   are slightly wider than the bottom margin
    C.   vary with the length of the letter
    D.   are figured independently from the letterhead and the body of the letter

Questions 16-20.

CODING

DIRECTIONS:

Name of Applicant	H A N G S B R U K E
Test Code	c o m p l e x i t y
File Number	0 1 2 3 4 5 6 7 8 9

Assume that each of the above capital letters is the first letter of the name of an Applicant, that the small letter directly beneath each capital letter is the test code for the Applicant, and that the number directly beneath each code letter is the file number for the Applicant.

In each of the following Questions 16 through 20, the test code letters and the file numbers in Columns 2 and 3 should correspond to the capital letters in Column 1. For each question, look at each column carefully and mark your answer as follows:

    If there is an error only in Column 2, mark your
    answer A.
    If there is an error only in Column 3, mark your
    answer B.
    If there is an error in both Columns 2 and 3, mark
    your answer C.
    If both Columns 2 and 3 are correct, mark your
    answer D.

The following sample question is given to help you understand the procedure.

SAMPLE QUESTION

Column 1	Column 2	Column 3
AKEHN	otyci	18902

In Column 2, the final test code letter *i*. should be *m*. Column 3 is correctly coded to Column 1. Since there is an error only in Column 2, the answer is A.

	Column 1	Column 2	Column 3	
16.	NEKKU	mytti	29987	16.____
17.	KRAEB	txyle	86095	17.____
18.	ENAUK	ymoit	92178	18.____
19.	REANA	xeomo	69121	19.____
20.	EKHSE	ytcxy	97049	20.____

Questions 21-30.

ARITHMETICAL REASONING

21. If a secretary answered 28 phone calls and typed the addresses for 112 credit state- ments in one morning, what is the ratio of phone calls answered to credit statements typed for that period of time?

21.__

    A. 1:4   B. 1:7   C. 2:3   D. 3:5

22. According to a suggested filing system, no more than 10 folders should be filed behind any one file guide and from 15 to 25 file guides should be used in each file drawer for easy finding and filing.
The maximum number of folders that a five-drawer file cabinet can hold to allow easy finding and filing is

22.__

    A. 550   B. 750   C. 1,100   D. 1,250

23. An employee had a starting salary of $25,804. He received a salary increase at the end of each year, and at the end of the seventh year his salary was $33,476.
What was his average annual increase in salary over these seven years?

23.__

    A. $1,020   B. $1,076   C. $1,096   D. $1,144

24. The 55 typists and 28 senior clerks in a certain city agency were paid a total of $1,943,200 in salaries last year.
If the average annual salary of a typist was $22,400 the average annual salary of a senior clerk was

24.__

    A. $25,400   B. $26,600   C. $26,800   D. $27,000

25. A typist has been given a three page report to type. She has finished typing the first two pages. The first page has 283 words, and the second page has 366 words.
If the total report consists of 954 words, how many words will she have to type on the third page of the report?

25.__

    A. 202   B. 287   C. 305   D. 313

26. In one day, Clerk A processed 30% more forms than Clerk B, and Clerk C processed li times as many forms as Clerk A. If Clerk B processed 40 forms, how many more forms were processed by Clerk C than Clerk B?

26.__

    A. 12   B. 13   C. 21   D. 25

27. A clerk who earns a gross salary of $452 every two weeks has the following deductions taken from her paycheck:
15% for City, State, Federal taxes; 2 1/2% for Social Security; $1.30 for health insur- ance; and $6.00 for union dues. The amount of her take-home pay is

27.__

    A. $256.20   B. $312.40   C. $331.60   D. $365.60

28. In 2005, a city agency spent $2,000 to buy pencils at a cost of $5.00 a dozen.
If the agency used 3/4 of these pencils in 2005 and used the same number of pencils in 2006, how many more pencils did it have to buy to have enough pencils for all of 2006?

28.__

    A. 1,200   B. 2,400   C. 3,600   D. 4,800

29. A clerk who worked in Agency X earned the following salaries: $20,140 the first year, $21,000 the second year, and $21,920 the third year. Another clerk who worked in Agency Y for three years earned $21,100 a year for two years and $21,448 the third year. The difference between the average salaries received by both clerks over a three-year period is

    A. $196   B. $204   C. $348   D. $564

29._____

30. An employee who works over 40 hours in any week receives overtime payment for the extra hours at time and one-half (1 1/2 times) his hourly rate of pay. An employee who earns $13.60 an hour works a total of 45 hours during a certain week.
His total pay for that week would be

    A. $564.40   B. $612.00   C. $646.00   D. $812.00

30._____

Questions 31-35.

RELATED INFORMATION

31. To tell a newly-employed clerk to fill a top drawer of a four-drawer cabinet with heavy folders which will be often used and to keep lower drawers only partly filled is

    A. *good,* because a tall person would have to bend unnecessarily if he had to use a lower drawer
    B. *bad,* because the file cabinet may tip over when the top drawer is opened
    C. *good,* because it is the most easily reachable drawer for the average person
    D. *bad,* because a person bending down at another drawer may accidentally bang his head on the bottom of the drawer when he straightens up

31._____

32. If a senior typist or senior clerk has requisitioned a *ream* of paper in order to duplicate a single page office announcement, how many announcements can be printed from the one package of paper?

    A. 200   B. 500   C. 700   D. 1,000

32._____

33. Your supervisor has asked you to locate a telephone number for an attorney named Jones, whose office is located at 311 Broadway, and whose name is not already listed in your files.
The BEST method for finding the number would be for you to

    A. call the information operator and have her get it for you
    B. look in the alphabetical directory (white pages) under the name Jones at 311 Broadway
    C. refer to the heading Attorney in the yellow pages for the name Jones at 311 Broadway
    D. ask your supervisor who referred her to Mr. Jones, then call that person for the number

33._____

34. An example of material that should NOT be sent by first class mail is a

    A. email copy of a letter   B. post card
    C. business reply card   D. large catalogue

34._____

35. In the operations of a government agency, a voucher is ORDINARILY used to   35.___

   A. refer someone to the agency for a position or assignment
   B. certify that an agency's records of financial trans-actions are accurate
   C. order payment from agency funds of a stated amount to an individual
   D. enter a statement of official opinion in the records of the agency

Questions 36-40.

ENGLISH USAGE

DIRECTIONS: Each question from 36 through 40 contains a sentence. Read each sentence carefully to decide whether it is correct. Then, in the space at the right, mark your answer:

   (A) if the sentence is incorrect because of bad grammar or sentence structure

   (B) if the sentence is incorrect because of bad punctuation

   (C) if the sentence is incorrect because of bad capitalization

   (D) if the sentence is correct

Each incorrect sentence has only one type of error. Consider a sentence correct if it has no errors, although there may be other correct ways of saying the same thing.

SAMPLE QUESTION I: One of our clerks were promoted yesterday.

The subject of this sentence is *one*, so the verb should be *was promoted* instead of *were promoted*. Since the sentence is incorrect because of bad grammar, the answer to Sample Question I is (A).

SAMPLE QUESTION II: Between you and me, I would prefer not going there.

Since this sentence is correct, the answer to Sample Question II is (D).

36. The National alliance of Businessmen is trying to persuade private businesses to hire   36.___
youth in the summertime.

37. The supervisor who is on vacation, is in charge of processing vouchers.   37.___

38. The activity of the committee at its conferences is always stimulating.   38.___

39. After checking the addresses again, the letters went to the mailroom.   39.___

40. The director, as well as the employees, are interested in sharing the dividends.   40.___

34

Questions 41-45.

FILING

DIRECTIONS: Each question from 41 through 45 contains four names. For each question, choose the name that should be FIRST if the four names are to be arranged in alphabeti-cal order in accordance with the Rules for Alphabetical Filing given below. Read these rules carefully. Then, for each question, indicate in the space at the right the letter before the name that should be FIRST in alphabet-ical order.

RULES FOR ALPHABETICAL FILING

Names of People

(1) The names of people are filed in strict alphabetical order, first according to the last name, then according to first name or initial, and finally according to middle name or initial. FOR EXAMPLE: George Allen comes before Edward Bell, and Leonard P. Reston comes before Lucille B. Reston.

(2) When last names are the same, FOR EXAMPLE, A. Green and Agnes Green, the one with the initial comes before the one with the name written out when the first initials are identical.

(3) When first and last names are alike and the middle name is given, FOR EXAMPLE, John David Doe and John Devoe Doe, the names should be filed in the alphabetical order of the middle names.

(4) When first and last names are the same, a name without a middle initial comes before one with a middle name or initial. FOR EXAMPLE, John Doe comes before both John A. Doe and John Alan Doe.

(5) When first and last names are the same, a name with a middle initial comes before one with a middle name beginning with the same initial. FOR EXAMPLE: Jack R. Hertz comes before Jack Richard Hertz.

(6) Prefixes such as De, O', Mac, Mc, and Van are filed as written and are treated as part of the names to which they are connected. FOR EXAMPLE: Robert O'Dea is filed before David Olsen.

(7) Abbreviated names are treated as if they were spelled out. FOR EXAMPLE: Chas. is filed as Charles and Thos. is filed as Thomas.

(8) Titles and designations such as Dr., Mr., and Prof, are disregarded in filing.

Names of Organizations

(1) The names of business organizations are filed according to the order in which each word in the name appears. When an organization name bears the name of a person, it is filed according to the rules for filing names of people as given above. FOR EXAMPLE: William Smith Service Co. comes before Television Distributors, Inc.

(2) *Where bureau, board, office, or department appears as the first part of the title of a governmental agency, that agency should be filed under the word in the title expressing the chief function of the agency. FOR EXAMPLE: Bureau of the Budget would be filed as if written Budget, (Bureau of the). The Department of Personnel would be filed as if written Personnel, (Department of).*

(3) *When the following words are part of an organization, they are disregarded: the, of, and.*

(4) *When there are numbers in a name, they are treated as if they were spelled out. FOR EXAMPLE: 10th Street Bootery is filed as Tenth Street Bootery.*

<u>SAMPLE QUESTION:</u>
    A. Jane Earl   (2)
    B. James A. Earle (4)
    C. James Earl   (1)
    D. J. Earle   (3)

The numbers in parentheses show the proper alphabetical order in which these names should be filed. Since the name that should be filed FIRST is James Earl, the answer to the Sample Question is (C).

41. A. Majorca Leather Goods   41.___
       B. Robert Maiorca and Sons
       C. Maintenance Management Corp.
       D. Majestic Carpet Mills

42. A. Municipal Telephone Service   42.___
       B. Municipal Reference Library
       C. Municipal Credit Union
       D. Municipal Broadcasting System

43. A. Robert B. Pierce   B. R. Bruce Pierce   43.___
       C. Ronald Pierce   D. Robert Bruce Pierce

44. A. Four Seasons Sports Club   B. 14th. St. Shopping Center   44.___
       C. Forty Thieves Restaurant   D. 42nd St. Theaters

45. A. Franco Franceschini   B. Amos Franchini   45.___
       C. Sandra Franceschia   D. Lilie Franchinesca

Questions 46-50.

SPELLING

DIRECTIONS: In each question, one of the words is misspelled. Select the letter of the misspelled word. *PRINT THE LETTER OF THE CORRECT ANSWER IN THE SPACE AT THE RIGHT.*

46. A. option   B. extradite   46.___
       C. comparitive   D. jealousy

47. A. handicaped   B. assurance   47.___
       C. sympathy   D. speech

48. A. recommend   B. carraige   48.____
     C. disapprove   D. independent

49. A. ingenuity   B. tenet (opinion)   49.____
     C. uncanny   D. intrigueing

50. A. arduous   B. hideous   50.____
     C. iervant   D. companies

KEY (CORRECT ANSWERS)

1. A	11. D	21. A	31. B	41. C
2. B	12. B	22. D	32. B	42. D
3. D	13. D	23. C	33. C	43. B
4. B	14. B	24. A	34. D	44. D
5. D	15. A	25. C	35. C	45. C
6. C	16. B	26. D	36. C	46. C
7. A	17. C	27. D	37. B	47. A
8. C	18. D	28. B	38. D	48. B
9. D	19. A	29. A	39. A	49. D
10. B	20. C	30. C	40. A	50. C'

EXAMINATION SECTION
TEST 1

DIRECTIONS: Each question or incomplete statement is followed by several suggested answers or completions. Select the one that *BEST* answers the question or completes the statement. *PRINT THE LETTER OF THE CORRECT ANSWER IN THE SPACE AT THE RIGHT.*

Questions 1-5.

DIRECTIONS: Each question from 1 to 5 consists of a sentence with an underlined word. For each question, select the choice that is *CLOSEST* in meaning to the underlined word.

EXAMPLE

This division reviews the fiscal reports of the agency.
In this sentence the word *fiscal* means most nearly
  A. financial   B. critical   C. basic   D. personnel
The correct answer is A. "financial" because "financial"
is closest to *fiscal*. Therefore, the answer is A.

1. Every good office worker needs basic skills.   1._____
   The word *basic* in this sentence means

   A. fundamental   B. advanced   C. unusual   D. outstanding

2. He turned out to be a good instructor.   2._____
   The word *instructor* in this sentence means

   A. student   B. worker   C. typist   D. teacher

3. The quantity of work in the office was under study.   3._____
   In this sentence, the word *quantity* means

   A. amount   B. flow   C. supervision   D. type

4. The morning was spent examining the time records.   4._____
   In this sentence, the word *examining* means

   A. distributing   B. collecting   C. checking   D. filing

5. The candidate filled in the proper spaces on the form.   5._____
   In this sentence, the word *proper* means

   A. blank   B. appropriate   C. many   D. remaining

Questions 6-8.

DIRECTIONS: You are to answer Questions 6 through 8 *SOLELY* on the basis of the information contained in the following paragraph:
The increase in the number of public documents in the last two centuries closely matches the increase in population in the United States. The great number of public documents has become a serious threat to their usefulness. It is necessary to have programs which will reduce the number of public documents that are kept and which will, at the same time, assure keeping those that have value. Such programs need a great deal of thought to have any success.

6. According to the above paragraph, public documents may be less useful if   6._

    A. the files are open to the public
    B. the record room is too small
    C. the copying machine is operated only during normal working hours
    D. too many records are being kept

7. According to the above paragraph, the growth of the population in the United States has   7._
matched the growth in the quantity of public documents for a period of, most nearly,

    A. 50 years   B.   100 years   C.   200 years   D.   300 years

8. According to the above paragraph, the increased number of public documents has made   8._
it necessary to

    A. find out which public documents are worth keeping
    B. reduce the great number of public documents by decreasing government services
    C. eliminate the copying of all original public documents
    D. avoid all new copying devices.

Questions 9-10.

DIRECTIONS: You are to answer Questions 9 and 10 SOLELY on the basis of the information
                contained in the following paragraph:
    The work goals of an agency can best be reached if the employees understand and agree
with these goals. One way to gain such understanding and agreement is for management to
encourage and seriously consider suggestions from employees in the setting of agency goals.

9. On the basis of the paragraph above, the BEST way to achieve the work goals of an   9._
agency is to

    A. make certain that employees work as hard as possible
    B. study the organizational structure of the agency
    C. encourage employees to think seriously about the agency's problems
    D. stimulate employee understanding of the work goals

10. On the basis of the paragraph above, understanding and agreement with agency goals   10._
can be gained by

    A. allowing the employees to set agency goals
    B. reaching agency goals quickly
    C. legislative review of agency operations
    D. employee participation in setting agency goals

Questions 11-15.

DIRECTIONS: Each of Questions 11 through 15 consists of a group of four words. One word
                in each group is INCORRECTLY spelled. For each question, print the letter of
                the correct answer in the space at the right that is the same as the letter next
                to the word which is INCORRECTLY spelled.
                                        EXAMPLE
    A.   housing   B.   certain   C.   budgit   D.   money

The word "budgit" is incorrectly spelled, because the correct spelling should be "budget."
Therefore, the correct answer is C.

11.	A.	sentince	B.	bulletin	C.	notice	D.	definition	11._____
12.	A.	appointment	B.	exactly	C.	typest	D.	light	12._____
13.	A.	penalty	B.	suparvise	C.	consider	D.	division	13._____
14.	A.	schedule	B.	accurate	C.	corect	D.	simple	14._____
15.	A.	suggestion	B.	installed	C.	proper	D.	agincy	15._____

Questions 16-20.

DIRECTIONS: Each question from 16 through 20 consists of a sentence which may be
  A.   incorrect because of bad word usage, or
  B.   incorrect because of bad punctuation, or
  C.   incorrect because of bad spelling, or
  D.   correct

Read each sentence carefully. Then print in the proper space at the right A, B, C, or D, according to the answer you choose from the four choices listed above. There is only one type of error in each incorrect sentence. If there is no error, the sentence is correct.

EXAMPLE

George Washington was the father of his contry.
This sentence is incorrect because of bad spelling ("contry" instead of "country"). Therefore, the answer is C.

16.   The assignment was completed in record time but the payroll for it has not yet been pre-   16._____
      parid.

17.   The operator, on the other hand, is willing to learn me how to use the mimeograph.   17._____

18.   She is the prettiest of the three sisters.   18._____

19.   She doesn't know; if the mail has arrived.   19._____

20.   The doorknob of the office door is broke.   20._____

21.   A clerk can process a form in 15 minutes. How many forms can that clerk process in six   21._____
      hours?

      A.   10   B.   21   C.   24   D.   90

22.   An office staff consists of 120 people. Sixty of them have been assigned to a special   22._____
      project. Of the remaining staff, 20 answer the mail, 10-handle phone calls, and the rest
      operate the office machines. The number of people operating the office machines is

      A.   20   B.   30   C.   40   D.   45

23.   An office worker received 65 applications but on the first day had to return 26 of them for   23._____
      being incomplete and on the second day 25 had to be returned for being incomplete.
      How many applications did not have to be returned?

      A.   10   B.   12   C.   14   D.   16

41

24. An office worker answered 63 phone calls in one day and 91 phone calls the next day. For these 2 days, what was the average number of phone calls he answered per day?

24.__

   A. 77   B. 28   C. 82   D. 93

25. An office worker processed 12 vouchers of $8.75 each, 3 vouchers of $3.68 each, and 2 vouchers of $1.29 each. The total dollar amount of these vouchers is

25.__

   A. $116.04   B. $117.52   C. $118.62   D. $119.04

———

KEY (CORRECT ANSWERS)

1.	A		11.	A
2.	D		12.	C
3.	A		13.	B
4.	C		14.	C
5.	B		15.	D
6.	D		16.	C
7.	C		17.	A
8.	A		18.	D
9.	D		19.	B
10.	D		20.	A

21.	C
22.	B
23.	C
24.	A
25.	C

———

TEST 2

Questions 1-5.

Mark your answer A if all the names are different
Mark your answer B if only two names are exactly the same
Mark your answer C if only three names are exactly the same
Mark your answer D if all four names are exactly the same

EXAMPLE

Jensen, Alfred E.
Jensen, Alfred E.
Jensan, Alfred E.
Jensen, Fred E.

Since the name Jensen, Alfred E. appears twice and is exactly the same in both places, the correct answer is B.

1. Riviera, Pedro S.   1.____
    Rivers, Pedro S.
    Riviera, Pedro N.
    Riviera, Juan S.

2. Guider, Albert   2.____
    Guidar, Albert
    Giuder, Alfred
    Guider, Albert

3. Blum, Rona   3.____
    Blum, Rona
    Blum, Rona
    Blum, Rona

4. Raugh, John   4.____
    Raugh, James
    Raughe, John
    Raugh, John

5. Katz, Stanley   5.____
    Katz, Stanley
    Katze, Stanley
    Katz, Stanley

Questions 6-10.

DIRECTIONS: Each Question 6 through 10 consists of numbers or letters in Columns I and II. For each question, compare each line of Column I with its corresponding line in Column II and decide how many lines in Column I are *EXACTLY* the same as their corresponding lines in Column II. In your answer space, mark your answer as follows:

Mark your answer A if only *ONE* line in Column I is exactly the same as its corresponding line in Column II
Mark your answer B if only *TWO* lines in Column I are exactly the same as their corresponding lines in Column II
Mark your answer C if only *THREE* lines in Column I are exactly the same as their corresponding lines in Column II
Mark your answer D if all *FOUR* lines in Column I are exactly the same as their corresponding lines in Column II

EXAMPLE

Column I	Column II
1776	1776
1865	1865
1945	1945
1976	1978

Only three lines in Column I are exactly the same as their corresponding lines in Column II. Therefore, the correct answer is C.

	Column I	Column II	
6.	5653	5653	6.
	8727	8728	
	ZPSS	ZPSS	
	4952	9453	
7.	PNJP	PNPJ	7.
	NJPJ	NJPJ	
	JNPN	JNPN	
	PNJP	PNPJ	
8.	effe	eFfe	8.
	uWvw	uWvw	
	KpGj	KpGg	
	vmnv	vmnv	
9.	5232	5232	9.
	PfrC	PfrN	
	zssz	zzss	
	rwwr	rwww	
10.	czws	czws	10.
	cecc	cece	
	thrm	thrm	
	lwtz	lwtz	

Questions 11-15.

DIRECTIONS: Questions 11 through 15 have lines of letters and numbers. Each letter should be matched with its number in accordance with the following table:

Letter	F	R	C	A	W	L	E	N	B	T
Matching Number	0	1	2	3	4	5	6	7	8	9

From the table you can determine that the letter F has the matching number 0 below it, the letter R has the matching number 1 below it, etc.

For each question, compare each line of letters and numbers carefully to see if each letter has its correct matching number. If all the letters and numbers are matched correctly in

none of the lines of the question, mark your answer A
only *one* of the lines of the question, mark your answer B
only *two* of the lines of the question, mark your answer C
all three lines of the question, mark your answer D

EXAMPLE

WBCR   4826
TLBF   9580
ATNE   3986

There is a mistake in the first line because the letter R should have its matching number 1 instead of the number 6.

The second line is correct because each letter shown has the correct matching number.

There is a mistake in the third line because the letter N should have the matching number 7 instead of the number 8,

Since all the letters and numbers are matched correctly in only one of the lines in the sample, the correct answer is B.

11.   EBCT   6829   11.____
          ATWR   3961
          NLBW   7584

12.   RNCT   1729   12.____
          LNCR   5728
          WAEB   5368

13.   NTWB   7948   13.____
          RABL   1385
          TAEF   9360

14.   LWRB   5417   14.____
          RLWN   1647
          CBWA   2843

15.   ABTC   3792   15.____
          WCER   5261
          AWCN   3417

16. Your job often brings you into contact with the public. Of the following, it would be MOST desirable to explain the reasons for official actions to people coming into your office for assistance because such explanations   16.

    A. help build greater understanding between the public and your agency
    B. help build greater self-confidence in city employees
    C. convince the public that nothing they do can upset a city employee
    D. show the public that city employees are intelligent

17. Assume that you strongly dislike one of your co-workers.
You should FIRST   17.

    A. discuss your feeling with the co-worker
    B. demand a transfer to another office
    C. suggest to your supervisor that the co-worker should be observed carefully
    D. try to figure out the reason for this dislike before you say or do anything

18. An office worker who has problems accepting authority is MOST likely to find it difficult to   18.

    A. obey rules   B. understand people
    C. assist other employees   D. follow complex instructions

19. The employees in your office have taken a dislike to one person and frequently annoy her. Your supervisor should   19.

    A. transfer this person to another unit at the first opportunity
    B. try to find out the reason for the staff's attitude before doing anything about it
    C. threaten to transfer the first person observed bothering this person
    D. ignore the situation

20. Assume that your supervisor has asked a worker in your office to get a copy of a report out of the files. You notice the worker has accidentally pulled out the wrong report.
Of the following, the BEST way for you to handle this situation is to tell   20.

    A. the worker about all the difficulties that will result from this error
    B. the worker about her mistake in a nice way
    C. the worker to ignore this error
    D. your supervisor that this worker needs more training in how to use the files

21. Filing systems differ in their efficiency. Which of the following is the BEST way to evaluate the efficiency of a filing system?
The   21.

    A. number of times used per day
    B. amount of material that is received each day for filing
    C. amount of time it takes to locate material
    D. type of locking system used

22. In planning ahead so that a sufficient amount of general office supplies is always available, it would be LEAST important to find out the   22.

    A. current office supply needs of the staff
    B. amount of office supplies used last year
    C. days and times that office supplies can be ordered
    D. agency goals and objectives

23. The *MAIN* reason for establishing routine office work procedures is that once a routine is   23.____
established

    A.   work need not be checked for accuracy
    B.   all steps in the routine will take an equal amount of time to perform
    C.   each time the job is repeated it will take less time to perform
    D.   each step in the routine will not have to be planned all over again each time

24. When an office machine centrally located in an agency must be shut down for repairs,   24.____
the bureaus and divisions using this machine should be informed of the

    A.   expected length of time before the machine will be in operation again
    B.   estimated cost of repairs
    C.   efforts being made to avoid future repairs
    D.   type of new equipment which the agency may buy in the future to replace the
        machine being repaired

25. If the day's work is properly scheduled, the *MOST* important result would be that the   25.____

    A.   supervisor will not have to do much supervision
    B.   employee will know what to do next
    C.   employee will show greater initiative
    D.   job will become routine

KEY (CORRECT ANSWERS)

1.	A		11.	C
2.	B		12.	B
3.	D		13.	D
4.	B		14.	B
5.	C		15.	A
6.	B		16.	A
7.	B		17.	D
8.	B		18.	A
9.	A		19.	B
10.	C		20.	B

21.	C
22.	D
23.	D
24.	A
25.	B

EXAMINATION SECTION
TEST 1

DIRECTIONS: Each question or incomplete statement is followed by several suggested answers or completions. Select the one that BEST answers the question or completes the statement. *PRINT THE LETTER OF THE CORRECT ANSWER IN THE SPACE AT THE RIGHT.*

1. Assume that a few co-workers meet near your desk and talk about personal matters during working hours. Lately, this practice has interfered with your work.
   In order to stop this practice, the BEST action for you to take FIRST is to

   A. ask your supervisor to put a stop to the co-workers' meeting near your desk
   B. discontinue any friendship with this group
   C. ask your co-workers not to meet near your desk
   D. request that your desk be moved to another location

   1.__

2. In order to maintain office coverage during working hours, your supervisor has scheduled your lunch hour from 1 P.M. to 2 P.M. and your co-worker's lunch hour from 12 P.M. to 1 P.M. Lately, your co-worker has been returning late from lunch each day. As a result, you don't get a full hour since you must return to the office by 2 P.M.
   Of the following, the BEST action for you to take FIRST is to

   A. explain to your co-worker in a courteous manner that his lateness is interfering with your right to a full hour for lunch
   B. tell your co-worker that his lateness must stop or you will report him to your supervisor
   C. report your co-worker's lateness to your supervisor
   D. leave at 1 P.M. for lunch, whether your co-worker has returned or not

   2.__

3. Assume that, as an office worker, one of your jobs is to open mail sent to your unit, read the mail for content, and send the mail to the appropriate person to handle. You accidentally open and begin to read a letter marked *personal* addressed to a co-worker.
   Of the following, the BEST action for you to take is to

   A. report to your supervisor that your co-worker is receiving personal mail at the office
   B. destroy the letter so that your co-worker does not know you saw it
   C. reseal the letter and place it on the co-worker's desk without saying anything
   D. bring the letter to your co-worker and explain that you opened it by accident

   3.__

4. Suppose that in evaluating your work, your supervisor gives you an overall good rating, but states that you sometimes turn in work with careless errors.
   The BEST action for you to take would be to

   A. ask a co-worker who is good at details to proofread your work
   B. take time to do a careful job, paying more attention to detail
   C. continue working as usual since occasional errors are to be expected
   D. ask your supervisor if she would mind correcting your errors

   4.__

5. Assume that you are taking a telephone message for a co-worker who is not in the office at the time.
   Of the following, the LEAST important item to write on the message is the

   A. length of the call   B. name of the caller
   C. time of the call   D. telephone number of the caller

   5.__

Questions 6-13.

DIRECTIONS: Questions 6 through 13 each consist of a sentence which may or may not be an example of good English. The underlined parts of each sentence may be correct or incorrect. Examine each sentence, considering grammar, punctuation, spelling, and capitalization. If the English usage in the underlined parts of the sentence given is better than any of the changes in the underlined words suggested in Options B, C, or D, choose Option A. If the changes in the underlined words suggested in Options B, C, or D would make the sentence correct, choose the correct option. Do not choose an option that will change the meaning of the sentence.

6. This Fall, the office will be closed on Columbus Day, October 9th.   6._____

    A. Correct as is
    B. fall...Columbus Day, October
    C. Fall...columbus day, October
    D. fall...Columbus Day, october

7. This manual discribes the duties performed by an Office Aide.   7._____

    A. Correct as is
    B. describe the duties performed
    C. discribe the duties performed
    D. describes the duties performed

8. There weren't no paper in the supply closet.   8._____

    A. Correct as is   B. weren't any
    C. wasn't any   D. wasn't no

9. The new employees left there office to attend a meeting.   9._____

    A. Correct as is   B. they're
    C. their   D. thier

10. The office worker started working at 8:30 a.m.   10._____

    A. Correct as is   B. 8:30 a.m.
    C. 8;30 a,m.   D. 8:30 am

11. The alphabet, or A to Z sequence are the basis of most filing systems.   11._____

    A. Correct as is
    B. alphabet, or A to Z sequence, is
    C. alphabet, or A to Z sequence are
    D. alphabet, or A too Z sequence, is

12. Those file cabinets are five feet tall.   12._____

    A. Correct as is   B. Them...feet
    C. Those...foot   D. Them...foot

13. The Office Aide checked the <u>register and finding</u> the date of the meeting.   13.

    A. Correct as is   B. regaster and finding
    C. register and found   D. regaster and found

Questions 14-21.

DIRECTIONS: Each of Questions 14 through 21 has two lists of numbers. Each list contains three sets of numbers. Check each of the three sets in the list on the right to see if they are the same as the corresponding set in the list on the left. Mark your answers:

    A. If none of the sets in the right list are the same as those in the left list
    B. if only one of the sets in the right list are the same as those in the left list
    C. if only two of the sets in the right list are the same as those in the left list
    D. if all three sets in the right list are the same as those in the left list

14. 7354183476   7354983476   14.
      4474747744   4474747774
      57914302311   57914302311

15. 7143592185   7143892185   15.
      8344517699   8344518699
      9178531263   9178531263

16. 2572114731   257214731   16.
      8806835476   8806835476
      8255831246   8255831246

17. 331476853821   331476858621   17.
      6976658532996   6976655832996
      3766042113715   3766042113745

18. 8806663315   8806663315   18.
      74477138449   74477138449
      211756663666   211756663666

19. 990006966996   99000696996   19.
      53022219743   53022219843
      4171171117717   4171171177717

20. 24400222433004   24400222433004   20.
      5300030055000355   5300030055500355
      20000075532002022   20000075532002022

21. 611166640660001116   61116664066001116   21.
      7111300117001100733   7111300117001100733
      26666446664476518   26666446664476518

Questions 22-25.

DIRECTIONS: Each of Questions 22 through 25 has two lists of names and addresses. Each list contains three sets of names and addresses. Check each of the three sets in the list on the right to see if they are the same as the corresponding set in the list on the left. Mark your answers:
- A. if none of the sets in the right list are the same as those in the left list
- B. if only one of the sets in the right list is the same as those in the left list
- C. if only two of the sets in the right list are the same as those in the left list
- D. if all three sets in the right list are the same as those in the left list

22. Mary T. Berlinger
2351 Hampton St.
Monsey, N.Y. 20117

Eduardo Benes
473 Kingston Avenue
Central Islip, N.Y. 11734

Alan Carrington Fuchs
17 Gnarled Hollow Road
Los Angeles, CA 91635

Mary T. Berlinger
2351 Hampton St.
Monsey, N.Y. 20117

Eduardo Benes
473 Kingston Avenue
Central Islip, N.Y. 11734

Alan Carrington Fuchs
17 Gnarled Hollow Road
Los Angeles, CA 91685

22.____

23. David John Jacobson
178 35 St. Apt. 4C
New York, N.Y. 00927

Ann-Marie Calonella
7243 South Ridge Blvd.
Bakersfield, CA 96714

Pauline M. Thompson
872 Linden Ave.
Houston, Texas 70321

David John Jacobson
178 53 St. Apt. 4C
New York, N.Y. 00927

Ann-Marie Calonella
7243 South Ridge Blvd.
Bakersfield, CA 96714

Pauline M. Thomson
872 Linden Ave.
Houston, Texas 70321

23.____

24. Chester LeRoy Masterton
152 Lacy Rd.
Kankakee, Ill. 54532

William Maloney
S. LaCrosse Pla.
Wausau, Wisconsin 52146

Cynthia V. Barnes
16 Pines Rd.
Greenpoint, Miss. 20376

Chester LeRoy Masterson
152 Lacy Rd.
Kankakee, Ill. 54532

William Maloney
S. LaCross Pla.
Wausau, Wisconsin 52146

Cynthia V. Barnes
16 Pines Rd.
Greenpoint, Miss. 20376

24.____

25. Marcel Jean Frontenac
6 Burton On The Water
Calender, Me. 01471

J. Scott Marsden
174 S. Tipton St.
Cleveland, Ohio

Lawrence T. Haney
171 McDonough St.
Decatur, Ga. 31304

Marcel Jean Frontenac
6 Burton On The Water
Calender, Me. 01471

J. Scott Marsden
174 Tipton St.
Cleveland, Ohio

Lawrence T. Haney
171 McDonough St.
Decatur, Ga. 31304

25.___

———

KEY (CORRECT ANSWERS)

1.	C	11.	B
2.	A	12.	A
3.	D	13.	C
4.	B	14.	B
5.	A	15.	B
6.	A	16.	C
7.	D	17.	A
8.	C	18.	D
9.	C	19.	A
10.	B	20.	C

21.	C
22.	C
23.	B
24.	B
25.	C

———

TEST 2

Questions 1-6.

DIRECTIONS: Questions 1 through 6 are to be answered SOLELY on the basis of the information contained in the following passage.

Duplicating is the process of making a number of identical copies of letters, documents, etc. from an original. Some duplicating processes make copies directly from the original document. Other duplicating processes require the preparation of a special master, and copies are then made from the master. Four of the most common duplicating processes are stencil, fluid, offset, and xerox.

In the stencil process, the typewriter is used to cut the words into a master called a stencil. Drawings, charts, or graphs can be cut into the stencil using a stylus. As many as 3,500 good-quality copies can be reproduced from one stencil. Various grades of finished paper from inexpensive mimeograph to expensive bond can be used.

The fluid process is a good method of copying from 50 to 125 good-quality copies from a master, which is prepared with a special dye. The master is placed on the duplicator, and special paper with a hard finish is moistened and then passed through the duplicator. Some of the dye on the master is dissolved, creating an impression on the paper. The impression becomes lighter as more copies are made; and once the dye on the master is used up, a new master must be made.

The offset process is the most adaptable office duplicating process because this process can be used for making a few copies or many copies. Masters can be made on paper or plastic for a few hundred copies, or on metal plates for as many as 75,000 copies. By using a special technique called photo-offset, charts, photographs, illustrations, or graphs can be reproduced on the master plate. The offset process is capable of producing large quantities of fine, top-quality copies on all types of finished paper.

The xerox process reproduces an exact duplicate from an original. It is the fastest duplicating method because the original material is placed directly on the duplicator, eliminating the need to make a special master. Any kind of paper can be used. The xerox process is the most expensive duplicating process; however, it is the best method of reproducing small quantities of good-quality copies of reports, letters, official documents, memos, or contracts.

1. Of the following, the MOST efficient method of reproducing 5,000 copies of a graph is   1._____

    A. stencil   B. fluid   C. offset   D. xerox

2. The offset process is the MOST adaptable office duplicating process because   2._____

    A. it is the quickest duplicating method
    B. it is the least expensive duplicating method
    C. it can produce a small number or large number of copies
    D. a softer master can be used over and over again

3. Which one of the following duplicating processes uses moistened paper?   3.__

    A. Stencil   B. Fluid   C. Offset   D. Xerox

4. The fluid process would be the BEST process to use for reproducing   4.__

    A. five copies of a school transcript
    B. fifty copies of a memo
    C. five hundred copies of a form letter
    D. five thousand copies of a chart

5. Which one of the following duplicating processes does NOT require a special master?   5.__

    A. Fluid   B. Xerox   C. Offset   D. Stencil

6. Xerox is NOT used for all duplicating jobs because   6.__

    A. it produces poor-quality copies
    B. the process is too expensive
    C. preparing the master is too time-consuming
    D. it cannot produce written reports

7. Assume a city agency has 775 office workers.   7.__
   If 2 out of 25 office workers were absent on a particular day, how many office workers reported to work on that day?

    A. 713   B. 744   C. 750   D. 773

Questions 8-11.

DIRECTIONS: In Questions 8 through 11, select the choice that is CLOSEST in meaning to the underlined word.

SAMPLE: This division reviews the fiscal reports of the agency.
    In this sentence, the word fiscal means MOST NEARLY
        A. financial   B. critical   C. basic   D. personnel

    The correct answer is A, financial, because financial is closest to fiscal.

8. A central file eliminates the need to retain duplicate material.   8.__
   The word retain means MOST NEARLY

    A. keep   B. change   C. locate   D. process

9. Filing is a routine office task.   9.__
   Routine means MOST NEARLY

    A. proper   B. regular   C. simple   D. difficult

10. Sometimes a word, phrase, or sentence must be deleted to correct an error.   10.__
    Deleted means MOST NEARLY

    A. removed   B. added   C. expanded   D. improved

11. Your supervisor will <u>evaluate</u> your work.
    <u>Evaluate</u> means MOST NEARLY

    A. judge   B. list   C. assign   D. explain

11.____

Questions 12-19.

DIRECTIONS: The code table below shows 10 letters with matching numbers. For each Question 12 through 19, there are three sets of letters. Each set of letters is followed by a set of numbers which may or may not match their correct letter according to the code table. For each question, check all three sets of letters and numbers and mark your answer:

        A.   if no pairs are correctly matched
        B.   if only one pair is correctly matched
        C.   if only two pairs are correctly matched
        D.   if all three pairs are correctly matched

<u>CODE TABLE</u>

T	M	V	D	S	P	R	G	B	H
1	2	3	4	5	6	7	8	9	0

<u>Sample Question:</u>   TMVDSP - 123456
                      RGBHTM - 789011
                      DSPRGB - 256789

In the sample question above, the first set of numbers correctly matches its set of letters. But the second and third pairs contain mistakes. In the second pair, M is incorrectly matched with number 1. According to the code table, letter M should be correctly matched with number 2. In the third pair, the letter D is incorrectly matched with number 2. According to the code table, letter D should be correctly matched with number 4. Since only one of the pairs is correctly matched, the answer to this sample question is B.

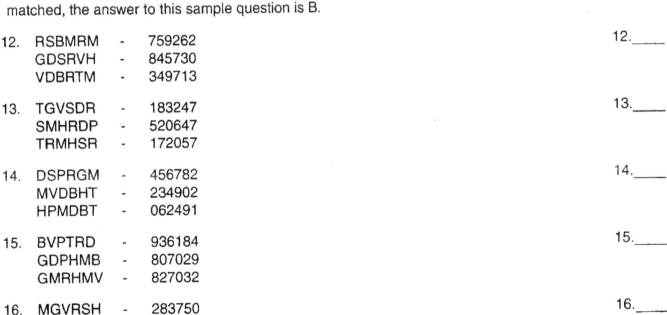

12. RSBMRM - 759262
      GDSRVH - 845730
      VDBRTM - 349713

12.____

13. TGVSDR - 183247
      SMHRDP - 520647
      TRMHSR - 172057

13.____

14. DSPRGM - 456782
      MVDBHT - 234902
      HPMDBT - 062491

14.____

15. BVPTRD - 936184
      GDPHMB - 807029
      GMRHMV - 827032

15.____

16. MGVRSH - 283750
      TRDMBS - 174295
      SPRMGV - 567283

16.____

17. SGBSDM - 489542
    MGHPTM - 290612
    MPBMHT - 269301

17.___

18. TDPBHM - 146902
    VPBMRS - 369275
    GDMBHM - 842902

18.___

19. MVPTBV - 236194
    PDRTMB - 647128
    BGTMSM - 981232

19.___

Questions 20-25.

DIRECTIONS: In each of Questions 20 through 25, the names of four people are given. For each question, choose as your answer the one of the four names given which should be filed FIRST according to the usual system of alphabetical filing of names, as described in the following paragraph.

In filing names, you must start with the last name. Names are filed in order of the first letter of the last name, then the second letter, etc. Therefore, BAILY would be filed before BROWN, which would be filed before COLT. A name with fewer letters of the same type comes first; i.e., Smith before Smithe. If the last names are the same, the names are filed alphabetically by the first name. If the first name is an initial, a name with an initial would come before a first name that starts with the same letter as the initial. Therefore, I. BROWN would come before IRA BROWN. Finally, if both last name and first name are the same, the name would be filed alphabetically by the middle name, one again an initial coming before a middle name which starts with the same letter as the initial. If there is no middle name at all, the name would come before those with middle initials or names.

Sample Question: A. Lester Daniels
                   B. William Dancer
                   C. Nathan Danzig
                   D. Dan Lester

The last names beginning with D are filed before the last name beginning with L. Since DANIELS, DANCER, and DANZIG all begin with the same three letters, you must look at the fourth letter of the last name to determine which name should be filed first. C comes before I or Z in the alphabet, so DANCER is filed before DANIELS or DANZIG. Therefore, the answer to the above sample question is B.

20.   A. Scott Biala   B. Mary Byala   20.___
      C. Martin Baylor   D. Francis Bauer

21.   A. Howard J. Black   B. Howard Black   21.___
      C. J. Howard Black   D. John H. Black

22.   A. Theodora Garth Kingston   B. Theadore Barth Kingston   22.___
      C. Thomas Kingston   D. Thomas T. Kingston

23.   A. Paulette Mary Huerta   B. Paul M. Huerta   23.___
      C. Paulette L. Huerta   D. Peter A. Huerta

24. A. Martha Hunt Morgan   B. Martin Hunt Morgan   24.____
     C. Mary H. Morgan   D. Martine H. Morgan

25. A. James T. Meerschaum   B. James M. Mershum   25.____
     C. James F. Mearshaum   D. James N. Meshum

KEY (CORRECT ANSWERS)

1.	C	11.	A
2.	C	12.	B
3.	B	13.	B
4.	B	14.	C
5.	B	15.	A
6.	B	16.	D
7.	A	17.	A
8.	A	18.	D
9.	B	19.	A
10.	A	20.	D

21.	B
22.	B
23.	B
24.	A
25.	C

TEST 3

Each question or incomplete statement is followed by several suggested answers or completions. Select the one that BEST answers the question or completes the statement. *PRINT THE LETTER OF THE CORRECT ANSWER IN THE SPACE AT THE RIGHT.*

1. Which one of the following statements about proper telephone usage is NOT always correct?
   When answering the telephone, you should

   A. know whom you are speaking to
   B. give the caller your undivided attention
   C. identify yourself to the caller
   D. obtain the information the caller wishes before you do your other work

1.___

2. Assume that, as a member of a worker's safety committee in your agency, you are responsible for encouraging other employees to follow correct safety practices. While you are working on your regular assignment, you observe an employee violating a safety rule.
   Of the following, the BEST action for you to take FIRST is to

   A. speak to the employee about safety practices and order him to stop violating the safety rule
   B. speak to the employee about safety practices and point out the safety rule he is violating
   C. bring the matter up in the next committee meeting
   D. report this violation of the safety rule to the employee's supervisor

2.___

3. Assume that you have been temporarily assigned by your supervisor to do a job which you do not want to do. The BEST action for you to take is to

   A. discuss the job with your supervisor, explaining why you do not want to do it
   B. discuss the job with your supervisor and tell her that you will not do it
   C. ask a co-worker to take your place on this job
   D. do some other job that you like; your supervisor may give the job you do not like to someone else

3.___

4. Assume that you keep the confidential personnel files of employees in your unit. A friend asks you to obtain some information from the file of one of your co-workers.
   The BEST action to take is to _____ to your friend.

   A. ask the co-worker if you can give the information
   B. ask your supervisor if you can give the information
   C. give the information
   D. refuse to give the information

4.___

Questions 5-8.

DIRECTIONS: Questions 5 through 8 are to be answered SOLELY on the basis of the information contained in the following passage.

City government is committed to providing a safe and healthy work environment for all city employees. An effective agency safety program reduces accidents by educating employees about the types of careless acts which can cause accidents. Even in an office, accidents can happen. If each employee is aware of possible safety hazards, the number of accidents on the job can be reduced.

Careless use of office equipment can cause accidents and injuries. For example, file cabinet drawers which are filled with papers can be so heavy that the entire cabinet could tip over from the weight of one open drawer.

The bottom drawers of desks and file cabinets should never be left open since employees could easily trip over open drawers and injure themselves.

When reaching for objects on a high shelf, an employee should use a strong, sturdy object such as a step stool to stand on. Makeshift platforms made out of books, papers, or boxes can easily collapse. Even chairs can slide out from under foot, causing serious injury.

Even at an employee's desk, safety hazards can occur. Frayed or cut wires should be repaired or replaced immediately. Computers which are not firmly anchored to the desk or table could fall, causing injury.

Smoking is one of the major causes of fires in the office. A lighted match or improperly extinguished cigarette thrown into a wastebasket filled with paper could cause a major fire with possible loss of life. Where smoking is permitted, ashtrays should be used. Smoking is particularly dangerous in offices where flammable chemicals are used.

5. The goal of an effective safety program is to

    A. reduce office accidents
    B. stop employees from smoking on the job
    C. encourage employees to continue their education
    D. eliminate high shelves in offices

5._____

6. Desks and file cabinets can become safety hazards when

    A. their drawers are left open
    B. they are used as wastebaskets
    C. they are makeshift
    D. they are not anchored securely to the floor

6._____

7. Smoking is especially hazardous when it occurs

    A. near exposed wires
    B. in a crowded office
    C. in an area where flammable chemicals are used
    D. where books and papers are stored

7._____

8. Accidents are likely to occur when

    A. employees' desks are cluttered with books and papers
    B. employees are not aware of safety hazards
    C. employees close desk drawers
    D. step stools are used to reach high objects

8._____

9. Assume that part of your job as a worker in the accounting division of a city agency is to answer the telephone. When you first answer the telephone, it is LEAST important to tell the caller   9.___

   A. your title
   C. the name of your unit

   B. your name
   D. the name of your agency

10. Assume that you are assigned to work as a receptionist, and your duties are to answer phones, greet visitors, and do other general office work. You are busy with a routine job when several visitors approach your desk.
The BEST action to take is to   10.___

   A. ask the visitors to have a seat and assist them after your work is completed
   B. tell the visitors that you are busy and they should return at a more convenient time
   C. stop working long enough to assist the visitors
   D. continue working and wait for the visitors to ask you for assistance

11. Assume that your supervisor has chosen you to take a special course during working hours to learn a new payroll procedure. Although you know that you were chosen because of your good work record, a co-worker, who feels that he should have been chosen, has been telling everyone in your unit that the choice was unfair.
Of the following, the BEST way to handle this situation FIRST is to   11.___

   A. suggest to the co-worker that everything in life is unfair
   B. contact your union representative in case your co-worker presents a formal grievance
   C. tell your supervisor about your co-worker's complaints and let her handle the situation
   D. tell the co-worker that you were chosen because of your superior work record

12. Assume that while you are working on an assignment which must be completed quickly, a supervisor from another unit asks you to obtain information for her.
Of the following, the BEST way to respond to her request is to   12.___

   A. tell her to return in an hour since you are busy
   B. give her the names of some people in her own unit who could help her
   C. tell her you are busy and refer her to a co-worker
   D. tell her that you are busy and ask her if she could wait until you finish your assignment

13. A co-worker in your unit is often off from work because of illness. Your supervisor assigns the co-worker's work to you when she is not there. Lately, doing her work has interfered with your own job.
The BEST action for you to take FIRST is to   13.___

   A. discuss the problem with your supervisor
   B. complete your own work before starting your co-worker's work
   C. ask other workers in your unit to assist you
   D. work late in order to get the jobs done

14. During the month of June, 40,587 people attended a city-owned swimming pool. In July, 13,014 more people attended the swimming pool than the number that had attended in June. In August, 39,655 people attended the swimming pool.
The TOTAL number of people who attended the swimming pool during the months of June, July, and August was

14.____

    A. 80,242   B. 93,256   C. 133,843   D. 210,382

Questions 15-22.

DIRECTIONS: Questions 15 through 22 test how well you understand what you read. It will be necessary for you to read carefully because your answers to these questions must be based ONLY on the information in the following paragraphs.

The telephone directory is made up of two books. The first book consists of the introductory section and the alphabetical listing of names section. The second book is the classified directory (also known as the yellow pages). Many people who are familiar with one book do not realize how useful the other can be. The efficient office worker should become familiar with both books in order to make the best use of this important source of information.

The introductory section gives general instructions for finding numbers in the alphabetical listing and classified directory. This section also explains how to use the telephone company's many services, including the operator and information services, gives examples of charges for local and long-distance calls, and lists area codes for the entire country. In addition, this section provides a useful postal zip code map.

The alphabetical listing of names section lists the names, addresses, and telephone numbers of subscribers in an area. Guide names, or *telltales*, are on the top corner of each page. These guide names indicate the first and last name to be found on that page. *Telltales* help locate any particular name quickly. A cross-reference spelling is also given to help locate names which are spelled several different ways. City, state, and federal government agencies are listed under the major government heading. For example, an agency of the federal government would be listed under *United States Government*.

The classified directory, or yellow pages, is a separate book. In this section are advertising services, public transportation line maps, shopping guides, and listings of businesses arranged by the type of product or services they offer. This book is most useful when looking for the name or phone number of a business when all that is known is the type of product offered and the address, or when trying to locate a particular type of business in an area. Businesses listed in the classified directory can usually be found in the alphabetical listing of names section. When the name of the business is known, you will find the address or phone number more quickly in the alphabetical listing of names section.

15. The introductory section provides

15.____

    A. shopping guides   B. government listings
    C. business listings   D. information services

16. Advertising services would be found in the

16.____

    A. introductory section   B. alphabetical listing of names section
    C. classified directory   D. information services

17. According to the information in the above passage for locating government agencies, the
    Information Office of the Department of Consumer Affairs of New York City government
    would be alphabetically listed FIRST under

    A. *I* for Information Offices
    B. *D* for Department of Consumer Affairs
    C. *N* for New York City
    D. *G* for government

17.

18. When the name of a business is known, the QUICKEST way to find the phone number is
    to look in the

    A. classified directory
    B. introductory section
    C. alphabetical listing of names section
    D. advertising service section

18.

19. The QUICKEST way to find the phone number of a business when the type of service a
    business offers and its address is known is to look in the

    A. classified directory
    B. alphabetical listing of names section
    C. introductory section
    D. information service

19.

20. What is a *telltale?*

    A. An alphabetical listing
    B. A guide name
    C. A map
    D. A cross-reference listing

20.

21. The BEST way to find a postal zip code is to look in the

    A. classified directory
    B. introductory section
    C. alphabetical listing of names section
    D. government heading

21.

22. To help find names which have several different spellings, the telephone directory pro-
    vides

    A. cross-reference spelling   B. *telltales*
    C. spelling guides   D. advertising services

22.

23. Assume that your agency has been given $2025 to purchase file cabinets.
    If each file cabinet costs $135, how many file cabinets can your agency purchase?

    A. 8   B. 10   C. 15   D. 16

23

24. Assume that your unit ordered 14 staplers at a total cost of $30.20, and each stapler cost   24._____
the same.
The cost of one stapler was MOST NEARLY

    A. $1.02   B. $1.61   C. $2.16   D. $2.26

25. Assume that you are responsible for counting and recording licensing fees collected by   25._____
your department. On a particular day, your department collected in fees 40 checks in the
amount of $6 each, 80 checks in the amount of $4 each, 45 twenty dollar bills, 30 ten dollar bills, 42 five dollar bills, and 186 one dollar bills.
The TOTAL amount in fees collected on that day was

    A. $1,406   B. $1,706   C. $2,156   D. $2,356

26. Assume that you are responsible for your agency's petty cash fund. During the month of   26._____
February, you pay out 7 $2.00 subway fares and one taxi fare for $10.85. You pay out
nothing else from the fund. At the end of February, you count the money left in the fund
and find 3 one dollar bills, 4 quarters, 5 dimes, and 4 nickels. The amount of money you
had available in the petty cash fund at the BEGINNING of February was

    A. $4.70   B. $16.35   C. $24.85   D. $29.55

27. You overhear your supervisor criticize a co-worker for handling equipment in an unsafe   27._____
way. You feel that the criticism may be unfair.
Of the following, it would be BEST for you to

    A. take your co-worker aside and tell her how you feel about your supervisor's com-
ments
    B. interrupt the discussion and defend your co-worker to your supervisor
    C. continue working as if you had not overheard the discussion
    D. make a list of other workers who have violated safety rules and give it to your
supervisor

28. Assume that you have been assigned to work on a long-term project with an employee   28._____
who is known for being uncooperative.
In beginning to work with this employee, it would be LEAST desirable for you to

    A. understand why the person is uncooperative
    B. act in a calm manner rather than an emotional manner
    C. be appreciative of the co-worker's work
    D. report the co-worker's lack of cooperation to your supervisor

29. Assume that you are assigned to sell tickets at a city-owned ice skating rink. An adult   29._____
ticket costs $4.50, and a children's ticket costs $2.25. At the end of a day, you find that
you have sold 36 adult tickets and 80 children's tickets.
The TOTAL amount of money you collected for that day was

    A. $244.80   B. $318.00   C. $342.00   D. $348.00

30. If each office worker files 487 index cards in one hour, how many cards can 26 office   30._____
workers file in one hour?

    A. 10,662   B. 12,175   C. 12,662   D. 14,266

KEY (CORRECT ANSWERS)

1.	D	16.	C
2.	B	17.	C
3.	A	18.	C
4.	D	19.	A
5.	A	20.	B
6.	A	21.	B
7.	C	22.	A
8.	B	23.	C
9.	A	24.	C
10.	C	25.	C
11.	C	26.	D
12.	D	27.	C
13.	A	28.	D
14.	C	29.	C
15.	D	30.	C

EXAMINATION SECTION

DIRECTIONS: Each question or incomplete statement is followed by several suggested answers or completions. Select the one that BEST answers the question or completes the statement. *PRINT THE LETTER OF THE CORRECT ANSWER IN THE SPACE AT THE RIGHT.*

Questions 1-15:
For each of the following questions, PRINT on the space at the right the word TRUE if the statement is true, or FALSE if the statement is false.

1. A typist who discovers an obvious grammatical error in a report she is typing should, under ordinary circumstances, copy the material as it was given to her.

1._____

2. The initials of the typist who typed a business letter generally appear on the letter.

2._____

3. It is considered POOR letter form to have *only* the complimentary close and the signature on the second page of a business letter.

3._____

4. Correspondence which is filed according to dates of letters is said to be filed chronologically.

4._____

5. It is *usually* unnecessary to proofread punctuation marks in a report.

5._____

6. The use of window envelopes *reduces* probability of mailing a letter to the wrong address.

6._____

7. Letter size paper is *usually* longer than legal size paper.

7._____

8. It is considered GOOD typing form to have two spaces following a comma.

8._____

9. Both sheets of a two-page typed letter MUST be letterheads.

9._____

10. Before removing a typed letter from the typewriter, the typist should read the copy so that corrections may be made neatly.

10._____

11. When alphabetizing names, you should ALWAYS disregard first names.

11._____

12. When filing a large number of cards according to the name on each card, it is generally a *good* procedure to alphabetize the cards FIRST.

12._____

13. When a report may be filed in a subject file under two headings, it is *good* practice to make a cross reference.

13._____

14. If an essential point has been omitted in a business letter, it is usually considered *good* letter form to include this point in a brief postscript.

14._____

15. Rough draft copies of a report should generally be single-spaced.

15._____

Questions 16-22:

The following items consist of problems in arithmetic. Print in the space at the right the word TRUE if the statement is true, and FALSE if the statement is false.

16. If the rate for first-class mail is 37 cents for each ounce or fraction of an ounce and 23 cents for each ounce or fraction of an ounce above one ounce, then the total cost of sending by first-class mail three letters weighing 1-1/2 ounces, 2 ounces, and 2-1/2 ounces, respectively, would be $1.80.

16._____

17. A typist, who in one hour typed a report consisting of five pages with 60 lines per page and 10 words per line, would have typed at the rate of 45 words per minute.

17._____

18. If a department store employs 45 clerks, 21 typists, and 18 stenographers, the percentage of these employees who are typists is 25%.

18._____

19. If four typists, who type at the same rate of speed, type 1,000 letters in 12 hours, then it will take six typists nine hours to type 1,000 letters.

19._____

20. If 15% of a stenographer's time is spent in taking dictation and 45% of her time is taken up in transcribing her notes, then she has a remainder of two-fifths of her time for performing other duties.

20._____

21. A typist completed 14 pages of a 24-page report before being asked to speak briefly with her employer, then typed the remaining 10 pages. Up until the time she spoke with her employer, the typist had already completed approximately 58% of the report.

21._____

22. Employee A types at a rate of 48 words per minute, while Employee B types at a rate of 54 words per minute. If both employees spend exactly 2-1/4 hours typing reports, Employee B will have typed approximately 810 more words than Employee A.

22._____

Questions 23-54:

Each of the following items consists of two words preceded by the letters A and B. In each item, *one* of the words may be spelled INCORRECTLY, or *both* words may be spelled CORRECTLY. If one of the words is spelled incorrectly, print in the space at the right the letter corresponding to the incorrect word. If both are spelled correctly, print the answer C.

23. A. accessible	B. artifical	23._____
24. A. feild	B. arranged	24._____
25. A. admittence	B. hastily	25._____
26. A. easely	B. readily	26._____
27. A. pursue	B. decend	27._____
28. A. measure	B. laboratory	28._____
29. A. exausted	B. traffic	29._____
30. A. discussion	B. unpleasant	30._____
31. A. campaign	B. murmer	31._____
32. A. guarantee	B. sanatary	32._____
33. A. communication	B. safty	33._____
34. A. numerus	B. celebration	34._____
35. A. nourish	B. begining	35._____
36. A. courious	B. witness	36._____
37. A. undoubtedly	B. thoroughly	37._____
38. A. justified	B. offering	38._____
39. A. predjudice	B. license	39._____
40. A. label	B. pamphlet	40._____
41. A. bulletin	B. physical	41._____
42. A. assure	B. exceed	42._____
43. A. advantagous	B. evident	43._____

44. A. benefit   B. occured   44. _____

45. A. acquire   B. graditude   45. _____

46. A. amenable   B. boundry   46. _____

47. A. deceive   B. voluntary   47. _____

48. A. imunity   B. conciliate   48. _____

49. A. acknoledge   B. presume   49. _____

50. A. substitute   B. prespiration   50. _____

51. A. reputible   B. announce   51. _____

52. A. luncheon   B. wretched   52. _____

53. A. regrettable   B. proficiency   53. _____

54. A. rescind   B. dissappoint   54. _____

Questions 55-72:
Each of the sentences that follow may be classified MOST appropriately under
one of the following three categories:
    A. *faulty* because of incorrect grammar
    B. *faulty* because of incorrect punctuation
    C. *correct*

Examine each sentence, then select the best answer as listed above and place
the letter in the space at the right. All incorrect sentences contain only ONE type
of error. Consider a sentence correct if it contains none of the types of errors
mentioned, even though there may be other correct ways of expressing the same
thought.

55. He sent the notice to the clerk who hired you yesterday.   55. _____

56. It must be admitted, however that you were not informed of this   56. _____
    change.

57. Only the employees who have served in this grade for at least two   57. _____
    years are eligible for promotion.

58. The work was divided equally between she and Mary.   58. _____

59. He thought that you were not available at the time.   59. _____

60. When the messenger returns; please give him this package.   60. _____

61. The new secretary prepared, typed, addressed, and delivered, the notices.

61. _____

62. Walking into the room, his desk can be seen at the rear.

62. _____

63. Although John has worked here longer then she, he produces a smaller amount of work.

63. _____

64. She said she could of typed this report yesterday.

64. _____

65. Neither one of these procedures are adequate for the efficient performance of this task.

65. _____

66. The typewriter is the tool of the typist; the cash register, the tool of the cashier.

66. _____

67. "The assignment must be completed as soon as possible" said the supervisor.

67. _____

68. As you know, office handbooks are issued to all new employees.

68. _____

69. Writing a speech is sometimes easier than to deliver it before an audience.

69. _____

70. Mr. Brown our accountant, will audit the accounts next week.

70. _____

71. Give the assignment to whomever is able to do it most efficiently.

71. _____

72. The supervisor expected either your or I to file these reports.

72. _____

Questions 73-90:
For each of the following test items, print the letter in the space at the right of the answer that BEST completes the statement.

73. A PREVALENT practice is one which is

73. _____

    A. rare   B. unfair   C. widespread   D. correct

74. To prepare a RECAPITULATION means *most nearly* to prepare a

74. _____

    A. summary   B. revision   C. defense   D. decision

75. An ADVERSE decision is one which is

75. _____

    A. unfavorable   B. unwise
    C. anticipated   D. backwards

76. A COMMENDATORY report is one which

76. _____

    A. expresses praise   B. contains contradictions
    C. is too detailed   D. is threatening

77. "The council will DEFER action on this matter." The word DEFER means *most nearly*

    A. hasten   B. consider   C. postpone   D. reject

77. _____

78. MEAGER results are those which are

    A. satisfactory   B. scant
    C. unexpected   D. praiseworthy

78. _____

79. An ARDUOUS job assignment

    A. requires much supervision   B. is laborious
    C. absorbs one's interest   D. is lengthy

79. _____

80. "This employee was IMPLICATED." The word IMPLICATED *most nearly* means

    A. demoted   B. condemned   C. involved   D. accused

80. _____

81. To be DETAINED means *most nearly* to be

    A. entertained   B. held back
    C. sent away   D. scolded

81. _____

82. An AMIABLE person is one who is

    A. active   B. pleasing   C. thrifty   D. foolish

82. _____

83. A UNIQUE procedure is one which is

    A. simple   B. uncommon   C. useless   D. ridiculous

83. _____

84. The word REPLENISH means *most nearly* to

    A. give up   B. punish   C. refill   D. empty

84. _____

85. A CONCISE report is one which is

    A. logical   B. favorable   C. brief   D. intelligent

85. _____

86. ELATED means *most nearly*

    A. lengthened   B. matured   C. excited   D. youthful

86. _____

87. SANCTION means *most nearly*

    A. approval   B. delay   C. priority   D. veto

87. _____

88. EGOTISTIC means *most nearly*

    A. tiresome   B. self-centered
    C. sly   D. smartly attired

88. _____

89. TRITE means *most nearly*

    A. brilliant   B. unusual
    C. funny   D. commonplace

89. _____

90. FESTIVE means *most nearly*

    A. edible   B. joyous   C. proud   D. serene

90. _____

KEY (CORRECT ANSWERS)

1. F	31. B	61. B
2. T	32. B	62. A
3. T	33. B	63. C
4. T	34. A	64. A
5. F	35. B	65. A
6. T	36. A	66. C
7. F	37. C	67. B
8. F	38. C	68. C
9. F	39. A	69. A
10. T	40. C	70. B
11. F	41. C	71. A
12. T	42. C	72. A
13. T	43. A	73. C
14. F	44. B	74. A
15. F	45. B	75. A
16. F	46. B	76. A
17. F	47. C	77. C
18. T	48. A	78. B
19. F	49. A	79. B
20. T	50. B	80. C
21. T	51. A	81. B
22. T	52. C	82. B
23. B	53. C	83. B
24. A	54. B	84. C
25. A	55. A	85. C
26. A	56. B	86. C
27. B	57. C	87. A
28. C	58. A	88. B
29. A	59. C	89. D
30. C	60. B	90. B

EXAMINATION SECTION
TEST 1

DIRECTIONS: Each question or incomplete statement is followed by several suggested answers or completions. Select the one that BEST answers the question or completes the statement. *PRINT THE LETTER OF THE CORRECT ANSWER IN THE SPACE AT THE RIGHT.*

Questions 1-30.

DIRECTIONS: In Questions 1 to 30, one word in each group is MISSPELLED. Indicate the letter of the error in the group.

1. A. aggrieve
    B. conceive
    C. beseige
    D. relieve

1.____

2. A. liege
    B. weird
    C. feign
    D. sieze

2.____

3. A. concede
    B. intercede
    C. precede
    D. supercede

3.____

4. A. chagrinned
    B. preferred
    C. changeable
    D. chargeable

4.____

5. A. therefor
    B. pastime
    C. oftimes
    D. allspice

5.____

6. A. forfeit
    B. glacier
    C. heifer
    D. feindish

6.____

7. A. filiament
    B. inferable
    C. soliloquy
    D. codeine

7.____

8. A. formidable
    B. impassible
    C. susceptible
    D. lamentible

8.____

73

9.   A   strategem
      B. reconnaissance
      C. mountainous
      D. consensus
                    9._

10.   A. attendent
      B. attorneys
      C. iridescence
      D. subterfuge
                    10._

11.   A. unparalleled
      B. sovereign
      C. indite
      D. heiroglyphic
                    11._

12.   A. pinnacle
      B. hypocrisy
      C. meridien
      D. palatable
                    12._

13.   A. maintainence
      B. ninety
      C. inoculate
      D. connoisseur
                    13._

14.   A. haranguing
      B. distilation
      C. unwieldy
      D. chandelier
                    14._

15.   A. glazier
      B. unrivalled
      C. triennial
      D. quintescence
                    15._

16.   A. stenciled
      B. similiar
      C. councilor
      D. gazetteer
                    16._

17.   A. receptable
      B. calsimine
      C. hideous
      D. mimicking
                    17._

18.   A. infringment
      B. abridgment
      C. symmetrical
      D. forgettable
                    18._

19.
A. naptha
B. vaccinate
C. chiffonier
D. annulling

19._____

20.
A. guise
B. guerilla
C. guage
D. guinea

20._____

21.
A. zigzagged
B. excelsior
C. maneuverable
D. effervesence

21._____

22.
A. reminiscence
B. stupify
C. embargoes
D. mosquitoes

22._____

23.
A. mistatement
B. occurrence
C. vanilla
D. allotted

23._____

24.
A. someone
B. requital
C. ecstasy
D. excize

24._____

25.
A. picayunish
B. colossal
C. interelatedness
D. rarefy

25._____

26.
A. dyeing
B. oscillatory
C. bouillion
D. lavalliere

26._____

27.
A. hieing
B. disasterous
C. ninetieth
D. cinnamon

27._____

28.
A. leisure
B. reconciliable
C. singeing
D. fetish

28._____

29.   A.   Chatanooga
      B.   Pittsburgh
      C.   Bismarck
      B.   Raleigh

29.__

30.   A.   supercilious
      B.   puntilious
      C.   sacrilegious
      D.   deleterious

30.__

Questions 31-50.

DIRECTIONS: Select the letter of the word or expression that MOST NEARLY expresses the
meaning of the capitalized word in the group.

31.   FECKLESS

31.__

   A.   spiritless   B.   supercilious
   C.   righteous   D.   unfeigned

32.   TIMOROUS

32.__

   A.   rash   B.   light-headed
   C.   wild   D.   timid

33.   PALPABLE

33.__

   A.   weak
   B.   tangible
   C.   trembling
   D.   foolish

34.   NUBILE

34.__

   A.   marriageable   B.   black
   C.   cloudy   D.   Numidian

35.   CANARD

35.__

   A.   game bird   B.   explosion
   C.   poltroon   D.   false story

36.   TENOR

36.__

   A.   purport   B.   kindness
   C.   effort   D.   serenity

37.   SCABROUS

37.__

   A.   rough   B.   itchy   C.   horrible   D.   crass

38.   SENTIENT

38.__

   A.   axiomatic   B.   contentious
   C.   authoritative   D.   capable of feeling

39. **RESTIVE**   39.____

   A. tired   B. estopped   C. uneasy   D. curious

40. **TRUNCATED**   40.____

   A. palmate   B. cut off   C. braced   D. stolid

41. **ROIL**   41.____

   A. render turbid
   B. amuse
   C. heat to high temperature
   D. ridicule

42. **ARROGATE**   42.____

   A. disparage   B. question
   C. claim presumptuously   D. accuse

43. **PALATINE**   43.____

   A. hilly   B. possessing royal privileges
   C. wan   D. huge

44. **ANOMALOUS**   44.____

   A. nameless   B. homeless   C. confusing   D. abnormal

45. **DOUR**   45.____

   A. dark   B. awesome   C. severe   D. angry

46. **REDOUBTABLE**   46.____

   A. unquestionable   B. arousing fear
   C. righteous   D. rash

47. **DEPRECATE**   47.____

   A. undervalue   B. plead against
   C. disparage   D. dispel

48. **SPLENETIC**   48.____

   A. captious   B. sumptuous
   C. febrile   D. fragmentary

49. **POLTERGEIST**   49.____

   A. type of rock   B. schemer
   C. beatnick   D. noisy spirit

50. **RIPOSTE**   50.____

   A. anger   B. clever retort
   C. strong hold   D. defeat

KEY (CORRECT ANSWERS)

1. C	11. D	21. D	31. A	41. A
2. D	12. C	22. B	32. B	42. C
3. D	13. A	23. A	33. B	43. B
4. A	14. B	24. D	34. A	44. D
5. C	15. D	25. C	35. D	45. C
6. D	16. B	26. D	36. A	46. B
7. A	17. B	27. B	37. A	47. B
8. D	18. A	28. B	38. D	48. A
9. A	19. A	29. A	39. C	49. D
10. A	20. C	30. B	40. B	50. B

———

TEST 2

DIRECTIONS: Each question or incomplete statement is followed by several suggested answers or completions. Select the one that BEST answers the question or completes the statement. *PRINT THE LETTER OF THE CORRECT ANSWER IN THE SPACE AT THE RIGHT.*

Questions 1-30.

DIRECTIONS: Select the letter of the word or expression that MOST NEARLY expresses the meaning of the capitalized word in the group.

1. COLLATE   1._____

   A. conflict   B. assemble
   C. disperse   D. add together

2. EFFRONTERY   2._____

   A. apprehension   B. deference
   C. temerity   D. incongruity

3. OBVIATE   3._____

   A. make unnecessary   B. make clear
   C. confound   D. oppose

4. LISSOM   4._____

   A. gay   B. frail   C. limber   D. apathetic

5. EXIGUOUS   5._____

   A. exceptional   B. outward
   C. leading   D. scanty

6. BROMIDIC   6._____

   A. trite   B. quaint   C. soothing   D. sluggish

7. NECROLOGY   7._____

   A. autopsy   B. enchantment
   C. magic   D. roll of dead

8. TENSILE   8._____

   A. ductile   B. strong
   C. delicate   D. pertaining to touch

9. IMPINGE   9._____

   A. irritate   B. puncture
   C. point at   D. infringe

10. CONDIGN   10._____

    A. gentle   B. offensive   C. trivial   D. deserved

11. LECTERN   11.

    A. lamp   B. throne
    C. reading desk   D. deacon

12. ALFRESCO   12.

    A. decorative   B. ill-mannered
    C. formal   D. open-air

13. EXORDIUM   13.

    A. casting out   B. introduction
    C. epilogue   D. termination

14. CONGERIES   14.

    A. eels   B. collection   C. innate   D. diseases

15. CONFLUENCE   15.

    A. meeting of rivers   B. power
    C. persuasion   D. harmony

16. PROTEA   16.

    A. equine   B. jutting out
    C. variable   D. stable

17. HISTRIONIC   17.

    A. pertaining to history
    B. artificial, affected
    C. concerning science of tissues
    D. graph of frequency distribution

18. BALLISTICS   18.

    A. intricate steps of dancers
    B. poems by unknown medieval writers
    C. pertaining to natives of Bali
    D. science of motion of projectiles

19. OBITER DICTUM   19.

    A. brief biographical sketch accompanying a death notice
    B. gravamen
    C. incidental opinion
    D. arbiter of fashion

20. FRENETIC   20.

    A. frenzied   B. refrigerated
    C. interlaced   D. characterized by noise

21. ORDNANCE   21.

    A. aircraft   B. fortifications
    C. decree   D. cannon or artillery

22. EXIGENT   22.____

    A. urgent   B. scanty
    C. obsolete   D. expelled by adjuration

23. EMPIRICAL   23.____

    A. pertaining to sovereignty
    B. of a large department store
    C. guided by experience
    D. celestial

24. ADVENTITIOUS   24.____

    A. risky   B. counterfeit
    C. inventive   D. accidental

25. DICHOTOMY   25.____

    A. cutting in two   B. ambiguous expression
    C. double entendre   D. tendency to digress

26. DISCRETE   26.____

    A. not orderly   B. subtle
    C. circumspect   D. distinct

27. DUODECIMAL   27.____

    A. expressed in the scale of twelve
    B. type of ulcer
    C. a twentieth portion
    D. a musical dialogue

28. ECUMENICAL   28.____

    A. metaphysical   B. universal
    C. heretical   D. non-clerical

29. FATUOUS   29.____

    A. pompous   B. inane   C. fleshy   D. inexact

30. NOISOME   30.____

    A. ear-splitting   B. uproarious
    C. noxious   D. teasing

Questions 31-50.

DIRECTIONS: In Questions 31 to 50, indicate the statement which is CORRECT according to
the standards of preferred English usage.

31. A. It is obvious that no one wants to be a kill-joy if they can help it.   31
     B. It is not always possible, and perhaps it never is possible, to judge a person's character by just looking at him.
     C. When Yogi Berra of the New York Yankees hit an immortal grand-slam home run, everybody in the huge stadium including Pittsburgh fans, rose to his feet.
     D. Every one of us students must pay tuition today.

32. A. The physician told the young mother that if the baby is not able to digest its milk, it   32
         should be boiled.
     B. There is no doubt whatsoever that he felt deeply hurt because John Smith had betrayed the trust.
     C. Having partaken of a most delicious repast prepared by Tessie Breen, the hostess, the horses were driven home immediately thereafter.
     D. The attorney asked my wife and myself several questions.

33. A. Despite all denials, there is no doubt in my mind that if my father were here you   33.
         wouldn't talk like that.
     B. At this time everyone must deprecate the demogogic attack made by one of our Senators on one of our most revered statesmen.
     C. In the first game of a crucial two-game series, Ted Williams, got two singles, both of them driving in a run.
     D. Our visitor brought good news to John and I.

34. A. If he would have told me, I should have been glad to help him in his dire financial   34.
         emergency.
     B. Newspaper men have often asserted that diplomats or so-called official spokesmen sometimes employ equivocation in attempts to deceive.
     C. I think someones coming to collect money for the Red Cross.
     D. In a masterly summation, the young attorney expressed his belief that the facts clearly militate against this opinion.

35. A. We have seen most all the exhibits.   35.
     B. Without in the least underestimating your advice, in my opinion the situation has grown immeasurably worse in the past few days.
     C. I wrote to the box office treasurer of the hit show that a pair of orchestra seats would be preferable.
     D. As the grim story of Pearl Harbor was broadcast on that fateful December 7, it was the general opinion that war was inevitable.

36. A. Without a moment's hesitation, Casey Stengel said that Larry Berra works harder   36.
         than any player on the team.
     A. There is ample evidence to indicate that many animals can run faster than any human being.
     B. No one saw the accident but I.
     C. Example of courage is the heroic defense put up by the paratroopers against overwhelming odds.

37. A. If you prefer these kind, Mrs. Grey, we shall be more than willing to let you have   37.
         them reasonably.
     B. If you like these here, Mrs. Grey, we shall be more than willing to let you have them reasonably.

C. If you like these, Mrs. Grey, we shall be more than willing to let you have them.
D. Who shall we appoint?

38.   A. The number of errors are greater in speech than in writing.   38.____
      B. The doctor rather than the nurse was to blame for his being neglected.
      C. Because the demand for these books have been so great, we reduced the price.
      D. John Galsworthy, the English novelist, could not have survived a serious illness; had it not been for loving care.

39.   A. Our activities this year have seldom ever been as interesting as they have been   39.____
this month.
      B. Our activities this month have been more interesting or at least as interesting as those of any month this year.
      C. Our activities this month has been more interesting than those of any other month this year.
      D. Neither Jean nor her sister was at home.

40.   A. George B. Shaw's view of common morality, as well as his wit sparkling with a dash 40.____
of perverse humor here and there, have led critics to term him *The Incurable Rebel.*
      B. The President's program was not always received with the wholehearted endorsement of his own party, which is why the party faces difficulty in drawing up a platform for the coming election.
      C. The reason why they wanted to travel was because they had never been away from home.
      D. Facing a barrage of cameras, the visiting celebrity found it extremely difficult to express his opinions clearly.

41.   A. When we calmed down, we all agreed that our anger had been kind of unneces- 41.____
sary and had not helped the situation.
      A. Without him going into all the details, he made us realize the horror of the accident.
      B. Like one girl, for example, who applied for two positions.
      C. Do not think that you have to be so talented as he is in order to play in the school orchestra.

42.   A. He looked very peculiarly to me.   42.____
      B. He certainly looked at me peculiar.
      C. Due to the train's being late, we had to wait an hour.
      D. The reason for the poor attendance is that it is raining.

43.   A. About one out of four own an automobile.   43.____
      B. The collapse of the old Mitchell Bridge was caused by defective construction in the central pier.
      C. Brooks Atkinson was well acquainted with the best literature, thus helping him to become an able critic.
      D. He has to stand still until the relief man comes up, thus giving him no chance to move about and keep warm.

44. A. He is sensitive to confusion and withdraws from people whom he feels are too noisy.
     B. Do you know whether the data is statistically correct?
     C. Neither the mayor or the aldermen are to blame.
     D. Of those who were graduated from high school, a goodly percentage went to college.

44.__

45. A. Acting on orders, the offices were searched by a designated committee.
     B. The answer probably is nothing.
     C. I thought it to be all right to excuse them from class.
     D. I think that he is as successful a singer, if not more successful, than Mary.

45.__

46. A. $90,000 is really very little to pay for such a well-built house.
     B. The creatures looked like they had come from outer space.
     C. It was her, he knew!
     D. Nobody but me knows what to do.

46.__

47. A. Mrs. Smith looked good in her new suit.
     B. New York may be compared with Chicago.
     C. I will not go to the meeting except you go with me.
     D. I agree with this editorial.

47.__

48. A. My opinions are different from his.
     B. There will be less students in class now.
     C. Helen was real glad to find her watch.
     D. It had been pushed off of her dresser.

48.__

49. A. Almost everyone, who has been to California, returns with glowing reports.
     B. George Washington, John Adams, and Thomas Jefferson, were our first presidents.
     C. Mr. Walters, whom we met at the bank yesterday, is the man, who gave me my first job.
     D. One should study his lessons as carefully as he can.

49.__

50. A. We had such a good time yesterday.
     B. When the bell rang, the boys and girls went in the schoolhouse.
     C. John had the worst headache when he got up this morning.
     D. Today's assignment is somewhat longer than yesterday's.

50.__

KEY (CORRECT ANSWERS)

1.	B	11.	C	21.	D	31.	D	41.	D
2.	C	12.	D	22.	A	32.	D	42.	D
3.	A	13.	B	23.	C	33.	B	43.	B
4.	C	14.	B	24.	D	34.	B	44.	D
5.	D	15.	A	25.	A	35.	D	45.	B
6.	A	16.	C	26.	D	36.	B	46.	D
7.	D	17.	B	27.	A	37.	C	47.	A
8.	A	18.	D	28.	B	38.	B	48.	A
9.	D	19.	C	29.	B	39.	D	49.	D
10.	D	20.	A	30.	C	40.	D	50.	D

CLERICAL ABILITIES TEST

Clerical aptitude involves the ability to perceive pertinent detail in verbal or tabular material, to observe differences in copy, to proofread words and numbers, and to avoid perceptual errors in arithmetic computation.

NATURE OF THE TEST

Four types of clerical aptitude questions are presented in the Clerical Abilities Test. There are 120 questions with a short time limit. The test contains 30 questions on name and number checking, 30 on the arrangement of names in correct alphabetical order, 30 on simple arithmetic, and 30 on inspecting groups of letters and numbers. The questions have been arranged in groups or cycles of five questions of each type. The Clerical Abilities Test is primarily a test of speed in carrying out relatively simple clerical tasks. While accuracy on these tasks is important and will be taken into account in the scoring, experience has shown that many persons are so concerned about accuracy that they do the test more slowly than they should. Competitors should be cautioned that speed as well as accuracy is important to achieve a good score.

HOW THE TEST IS ADMINISTERED

Each competitor should be given a copy of the test booklet with sample questions on the cover page, an answer sheet, and a medium No. 2 pencil. Ten minutes are allowed to study the directions and sample questions and to answer the questions in the proper boxes on the two pages.

The separate answer sheet should be used for the test proper. Fifteen minutes are allowed for the test.

HOW THE TEST IS SCORED

The correct answers should be counted and recorded. The number of incorrect answers must also be counted because one-fourth of the number of incorrect answers is subtracted from the number of right answers. An omission is considered as neither a right nor a wrong answer. The score on this test is the number of right answers minus one-fourth of the number of wrong answers (fractions of one-half or less are dropped). For example, if an applicant had answered 89 questions correctly and 10 questions incorrectly, and had omitted 1 question, his score would be 87.

EXAMINATION SECTION

DIRECTIONS: This test contains four kinds of questions. There are some of each kind on each page in the booklet. The time limit for the test will be announced by the examiner.

Use the special pencil furnished by the examiner in marking your answers on the separate answer sheet. For each question, there are five suggested answers. Decide which answer is correct, find the number of the question on the answer sheet, and make a *solid black mark* between the dotted lines just below the letter of your answer. If you wish to change your answer, erase the first mark completely—do not merely cross it out.

SAMPLE QUESTIONS

In each line across the page there are three names or numbers that are much alike. Compare the three names or numbers and decide which ones are exactly alike. On the Sample Answer Sheet at the right, mark the answer-

A   if ALL THREE names or numbers are exactly ALIKE
B   if only the FIRST and SECOND names or numbers are exactly ALIKE
C   if only the FIRST and THIRD names or numbers are exactly ALIKE
D   if only the SECOND and THIRD names or numbers are exactly ALIKE
E   if ALL THREE names or numbers are DIFFERENT

I.	Davis Hazen	David Hozen	David Hazen
II.	Lois Appel	Lois Appel	Lois Apfel
III.	June Allan	Jane Allan	Jane Allan
IV.	10235	10235	10235
V.	32614	32164	32614

It will be to your advantage to learn what A, B, C, D, and E stand for. If you finish the sample questions before you are told to turn to the test, study them.

	SAMPLE ANSWER SHEET				
	A	B	C	D	E
I					
II					
III					
IV					
V					
VI					
VII					

In the next group of sample questions, there is a name in a box at the left, and four other names in alphabetical order at the right. Find the correct space for the boxed name so that it will be in alphabetical order with the others, and mark the letter of that space as your answer.

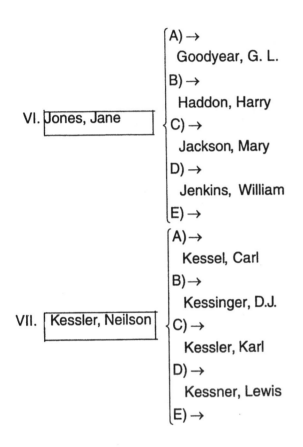

VI. Jones, Jane

A) →
  Goodyear, G. L.
B) →
  Haddon, Harry
C) →
  Jackson, Mary
D) →
  Jenkins, William
E) →

VII. Kessler, Neilson

A) →
  Kessel, Carl
B) →
  Kessinger, D.J.
C) →
  Kessler, Karl
D) →
  Kessner, Lewis
E) →

CORRECT ANSWERS TO.
SAMPLE QUESTIONS

	A	B	C	D	E
I					▌
II		▌			
III				▌	
IV	▌				
V			▌		
VI					▌
VII				▌	

DIRECTIONS: In the following questions, complete the equation and find your answer among the list of suggested answers. Mark the Sample Answer Sheet A, B, C or D for the answer you obtained; or if your answer is not among these, mark E for that question.

VIII. Add:

    22   A) 44 B) 45
  + 33   C) 54 D) 55
            E) none of these

IX. Subtract:

    24   A) 20 B) 21
  − 3   C) 27 D) 29
            E) none of these

X. Multiply:

    25   A) 100 B) 115
  x 5   C) 125 D) 135
            E) none of these

XI. Divide:

            A) 20 B) 22
  6 / 126   C) 24 D) 26
            E) none of these

Directions: There is one set of suggested answers for the next group of sample questions. Do not try to memorize these answers, because there will be a different set on each page in the test.

To find the answer to a question, find which suggested answer contains numbers and letters all of which appear in the question. If no suggested answer fits, mark E for that question.

XII.   8NK9GT46
XIII. T97Z6L3K
XIV.   Z7GK398N
XV.   3K946GZL
XVI.   ZN738KT9

Suggested Answers
A = 7,9,G,K
B = 8,9,T,Z
C = 6,7,K,Z
D = 6,8,G,T
E = none of these

SAMPLE ANSWER SHEET						CORRECT ANSWERS TO SAMPLE QUESTIONS				
	A	B	C	D	E	A	B	C	D	E
VIII									■	
IX							■			
X								■		
XI										■
XII									■	
XIII								■		
XIV						■				
XV										■
XVI							■			

After you have marked your answers to all the questions on the Sample Answer Sheets on this page and on the front page of the booklet, check them with the answers in the boxes marked Correct Answers to Sample Questions.

In questions 1 through 5, compare the three names or numbers, and mark

A   if ALL THREE names or numbers are exactly ALIKE
B   if only the FIRST and SECOND names or numbers are exactly ALIKE
C   if only the FIRST and THIRD names or numbers are exactly ALIKE
D   if only the SECOND and THIRD names or numbers are exactly ALIKE
E   if ALL THREE names or numbers are DIFFERENT

1.	5261383	5261383	5261338
2.	8125690	8126690	8125609
3.	W. E. Johnston	W. E. Johnson	W. E. Johnson
4.	Vergil L. Muller	Vergil L. Muller	Vergil L. Muller
5.	Atherton R. Warde	Asheton R. Warde	Atherton P. Warde

In questions 6 through 10, find the correct place for the name in the box.

6. **Hackett, Gerald**

A) →
Habert, James
B) →
Hachett, J. J.
C) →
Hachetts, K, Larson
D) →
Hachettson, Leroy
E) →

7. **Margenroth, Alvin**

A) →
Margeroth, Albert
B) →
Margestein, Dan
C) →
Margestein, David
D) →
Margue, Edgar
E) →

8. **Bobbitt, Olivier E.**

A) →
Bobbitt, D. Olivier
B) →
Bobbitt, Olive B.
C) →
Bobbitt, Olivia H.
D) →
Bobbitt, R. Olivia
E) →

9. **Mosely, Werner**

A) →
Mosely, Albert J.
B) →
Mosley, Alvin
C) →
Mosley, S. M.
D) →
Mozley, Vinson N.
E) →

10. **Youmuns, Frank L.**

A) →
Youmons, Frank G.
B) →
Youmons, Frank H.
C) →
Youmons, Frank K.
D) →
Youmons, Frank M.
E) →

GO ON TO THE NEXT COLUMN.

Answers

→ 11. Add:

$$\begin{array}{r} 4\ 3 \\ +\ 3\ 2 \\ \hline \end{array}$$

A) 55   B) 65
C) 66   D) 75
E) none of these

12. Subtract:

$$\begin{array}{r} 8\ 3 \\ -\quad 4 \\ \hline \end{array}$$

A) 73   B) 79
C) 80   D) 89
E) none of these

13. Multiply:

$$\begin{array}{r} 4\ 1 \\ \times\quad 7 \\ \hline \end{array}$$

A) 281   B) 287
C) 291   D) 297
E) none of these

14. Divide:

$$6\ /\ \overline{3\ 0\ 6}$$

A) 44   B) 51
C) 52   D) 60
E) none of these

15. Add:

$$\begin{array}{r} 3\ 7 \\ +\ 1\ 5 \\ \hline \end{array}$$

A) 42   B) 52
C) 53   D) 62
E) none of these

For each question below, find which one of the suggested answers appears in that question.

16.   6 2 5 K 4 P T G

17.   L 4 7 2 T 6 V K

18.   3 5 4 L 9 V T G

19.   G 4 K 7 L 3 5 Z

20.   4 K 2 9 N 5 T G

Suggested Answers

A=4, 5, K, T
B=4, 7, G, K
C=2, 5, G, L
D=2, 7, L, T
E=none of these

GO ON TO THE NEXT PAGE.

In questions 21 through 25, compare the three names or numbers, and mark the answer

A if ALL THREE names or numbers are exactly ALIKE
B if only the FIRST and SECOND names or numbers are exactly ALIKE
C if only the FIRST and THIRD names or numbers are exactly ALIKE
D if only the SECOND and THIRD names or numbers are exactly ALIKE
E if ALL THREE names or numbers are DIFFERENT

21. 2395890	2395890	2395890
22. 1926341	1926347	1926314
23. E. Owens McVey	E. Owen McVey	E. Owen McVay
24. Emily Neal Rouse	Emily Neal Rowse	Emily Neal Rowse
25. H. Merritt Audubon	H. Merriott Audubon	H. Merritt Audubon

In questions 26 through 30, find the correct place for the name in the box.

26. | Watters, N. O. |

A) →
  Waters, Charles L.
B) →
  Waterson, Nina P.
C) →
  Watson, Nora J.
D) →
  Wattwood, Paul A.
E) →

27. | Johnston, Edward |

A) →
  Johnston, Edgar R.
B) →
  Johnston, Edmond
C) →
  Johnston, Edmund
D) →
  Johnstone, Edmund A.
E) →

28. | Rensch, Adeline |

A) →
  Ramsay, Amos
B) →
  Remschel, Augusta
C) →
  Renshaw, Austin
D) →
  Rentzel, Becky
E) →

29. | Schnyder, Maurice |

A) →
  Schneider, Martin
B) →
  Schneider, Mertens
C) →
  Schnyder, Newman
D) →
  Schreibner, Norman
E) →

30. | Freedenburg, C. Erma |

A) →
  Freedenberg, Emerson
B) →
  Freedenberg, Erma
C) →
  Freedenberg, Erma E.
D) →
  Freedinberg, Erma F.
E) →

GO ON TO THE NEXT COLUMN.

Answers

31. Subtract:
  6 8
  − 4 7
  ——
  A) 10   B) 11
  C) 20   D) 22
  E) none of these

32. Multiply:
  5 0
  × 8
  ——
  A) 400   B) 408
  C) 450   D) 458
  E) none of these

33. Divide:
  9 / 1 8 0
  A) 20   B) 29
  C) 30   D) 39
  E) none of these

34. Add:
  7 8
  + 6 3
  ——
  A) 131   B) 140
  C) 141   D) 151
  E) none of these

35. Subtract:
  8 9
  − 7 0
  ——
  A) 9   B) 18
  C) 19   D) 29
  E) none of these

For each question below, find which one of the suggested answers appears in that question.

36. 9 G Z 3 L 4 6 N

37. L 5 N K 4 3 9 V

38. 8 2 V P 9 L Z 5

39. V P 9 Z 5 L 8 7

40. 5 T 8 N 2 9 V L

Suggested Answers
  A = 4, 9, L, V
  B = 4, 5, N, Z
  C = 5, 8, L, Z
  D = 8, 9, N, V
  E = none of these

GO ON TO THE NEXT PAGE.

In questions 41 through 45, compare the three names or numbers, and mark the answer
  A if ALL THREE names or numbers are exactly ALIKE
  B if only the FIRST and SECOND names or numbers are exactly ALIKE
  C if only the FIRST and THIRD names or numbers are exactly ALIKE
  D if only the SECOND and THIRD names or numbers are exactly ALIKE
  E if ALL THREE names or numbers are DIFFERENT

41.	6219354	6219354	6219354
42.	2312793	2312793	2312793
43.	1065407	1065407	1065047
44.	Francis Ransdell	Frances Ramsdell	Francis Ramsdell
45.	Cornelius Detwiler	Cornelius Detwiler	Cornelius Detwiler

In questions 46 through 50, find the correct place for the name in the box.

46. DeMattia, Jessica
A) →
DeLong, Jesse
B) →
DeMatteo, Jessie
C) →
Derby, Jessie S.
D) →
DeShazo, L. M.
E) →

47. Theriault, Louis
A) →
Therien, Annette
B) →
Therien, Elaine
C) →
Thibeault, Gerald
D) →
Thiebeault, Pierre
E) →

48. Gaston, M. Hubert
A) →
Gaston, Dorothy M.
B) →
Gaston, Henry N.
C) →
Gaston, Isabel
D) →
Gaston, M. Melvin
E) →

49. SanMiguel, Carlos
A) →
SanLuis, Juana
B) →
Santilli, Laura
C) →
Stinnett, Nellie
D) →
Stoddard, Victor
E) →

50. DeLaTour, Hall F.
A) →
Delargy, Harold
B) →
DeLathouder, Hilda
C) →
Lathrop, Hillary
D) →
LaTour, Hulbert E.
E) →

Answers

51. Multiply:
6 2
× 5
A) 300 B) 310
C) 315 D) 360
E) none of these

52. Divide:
3 / 1 5 3
A) 41 B) 43
C) 51 D) 53
E) none of these

53. Add:
4 7
+ 2 1
A) 58 B) 59
C) 67 D) 68
E) none of these

54. Subtract:
8 7
− 4 2
A) 34 B) 35
C) 44 D) 45
E) none of these

55. Multiply:
3 7
× 3
A) 91   B) 101
C) 104 D) 114
E) none of these

For each question below, find which one of the suggested answers appears in that question.

56. N 5 4 7 T K 3 Z

57. 8 5 3 V L 2 Z N

58. 7 2 5 N 9 K L V

59. 9 8 L 2 5 Z K V

60. Z 6 5 V 9 3 P N

Suggested Answers
A=3, 8, K, N
B=5, 8, N, V
C=3, 9, V, Z
D=5, 9, K, Z
E=none of these

GO ON TO THE NEXT COLUMN. **GO ON TO THE NEXT PAGE.**

93

8

In questions 61 through 65, compare the three names or numbers, and mark the answer

A   if ALL THREE names or numbers are exactly ALIKE
B   if only the FIRST and SECOND names or numbers are exactly ALIKE
C   if only the FIRST and THIRD names or numbers are exactly ALIKE
D   if only the SECOND and THIRD names or numbers are exactly ALIKE
E   if ALL THREE names or numbers are DIFFERENT

61. 6452054   6452654   6452054
62. 8501268   8501268   8501286
63. Ella Burk Newham   Ella Burk Newnham Elena Burk Newnham
64. Jno. K. Ravencroft Jno. H. Ravencroft Jno. H. Ravencoft
65. Martin Wills Pullen Martin Wills Pulen Martin Wills Pullen

In questions 66 through 70, find the correct place for the name in the box.

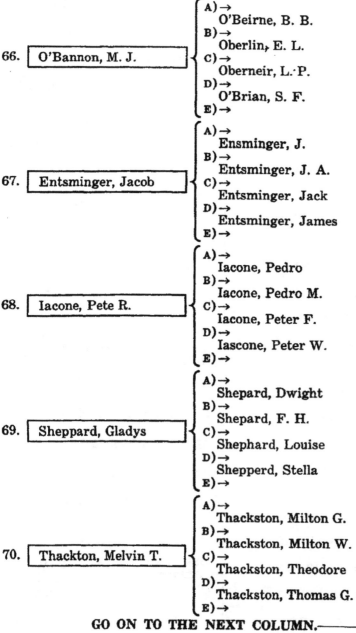

66. O'Bannon, M. J.
  A)→ O'Beirne, B. B.
  B)→ Oberlin, E. L.
  C)→ Oberneir, L. P.
  D)→ O'Brian, S. F.
  E)→

67. Entsminger, Jacob
  A)→ Ensminger, J.
  B)→ Entsminger, J. A.
  C)→ Entsminger, Jack
  D)→ Entsminger, James
  E)→

68. Iacone, Pete R.
  A)→ Iacone, Pedro
  B)→ Iacone, Pedro M.
  C)→ Iacone, Peter F.
  D)→ Iascone, Peter W.
  E)→

69. Sheppard, Gladys
  A)→ Shepard, Dwight
  B)→ Shepard, F. H.
  C)→ Shephard, Louise
  D)→ Shepperd, Stella
  E)→

70. Thackton, Melvin T.
  A)→ Thackston, Milton G.
  B)→ Thackston, Milton W.
  C)→ Thackston, Theodore
  D)→ Thackston, Thomas G.
  E)→

GO ON TO THE NEXT COLUMN.

Answers

71. Divide: 7 / 3 5 7
   A) 51 B) 52 C) 53 D) 54 E) none of these

72. Add: 5 8 + 2 7
   A) 75 B) 84 C) 85 D) 95 E) none of these

73. Subtract: 8 6 − 5 7
   A) 18 B) 29 C) 38 D) 39 E) none of these

74. Multiply: 6 8 × 4
   A) 242 B) 264 C) 272 D) 274 E) none of these

75. Divide: 9 / 6 3 9
   A) 71 B) 73 C) 81 D) 83 E) none of these

For each question below, find which one of the suggested answers appears in that question.

76. 6 Z T N 8 7 4 V

77. V 7 8 6 N 5 P L

78. N 7 P V 8 4 2 L

79. 7 8 G 4 3 V L T

80. 4 8 G 2 T N 6 L

Suggested Answers
A = 2, 7, L, N
B = 2, 8, T, V
C = 6, 8, L, T
D = 6, 7, N, V
E = none of these

GO ON TO THE NEXT PAGE.

94

In questions 81 through 85, compare the three names or numbers, and mark the answer
- A   if ALL THREE names or numbers are exactly ALIKE
- B   if only the FIRST and SECOND names or numbers are exactly ALIKE
- C   if only the FIRST and THIRD names or numbers are exactly ALIKE
- D   if only the SECOND and THIRD names or numbers are exactly ALIKE
- E   if ALL THREE names or numbers are DIFFERENT

81. 3457988	3457986	3457986
82. 4695682	4695862	4695682
83. Stricklund Kanedy	Stricklund Kanedy	Stricklund Kanedy
84. Joy Harlor Witner	Joy Harloe Witner	Joy Harloe Witner
85. R. M.O. Uberroth	R. M.O. Uberroth	R. N.O. Uberroth

In questions 86 through 90, find the correct place for the name in the box.

86. Dunlavey, M. Hilary
- A)→ Dunleavy, Hilary G.
- B)→ Dunleavy, Hilary K.
- C)→ Dunleavy, Hilary S.
- D)→ Dunleavy, Hilery W.
- E)→

87. Yarbrough, Maria
- A)→ Yabroudy, Margy
- B)→ Yarboro, Marie
- C)→ Yarborough, Marina
- D)→ Yarborough, Mary
- E)→

88. Prouty, Martha
- A)→ Proutey, Margaret
- B)→ Proutey, Maude
- C)→ Prouty, Myra
- D)→ Prouty, Naomi
- E)→

89. Pawlowicz, Ruth M.
- A)→ Pawalek, Edward
- B)→ Pawelek, Flora G.
- C)→ Pawlowski, Joan M.
- D)→ Pawtowski, Wanda
- E)→

90. Vanstory, George
- A)→ Vanover, Eva
- B)→ VanSwinderen, Floyd
- C)→ VanSyckle, Harry
- D)→ Vanture, Laurence
- E)→

Answers

91. Add: 2 8 + 3 5
A) 53 B) 62 C) 64 D) 73 E) none of these

92. Subtract: 7 8 − 6 9
A) 7 B) 8 C) 18 D) 19 E) none of these

93. Multiply: 8 6 × 6
A) 492 B) 506 C) 516 D) 526 E) none of these

94. Divide: 8 / 6 4 8
A) 71 B) 76 C) 81 D) 89 E) none of these

95. Add: 9 7 + 3 4
A) 131 B) 132 C) 140 D) 141 E) none of these

For each question below, find which one of the suggested answers appears in that question.

96. V 5 7 Z N 9 4 T

97. 4 6 P T 2 N K 9

98. 6 4 N 2 P 8 Z K

99. 7 P 5 2 4 N K T

100. K T 8 5 4 N 2 P

Suggested Answers
- A=2, 5, N, Z
- B=4, 5, N, P
- C=2, 9, P, T
- D=4, 9, T, Z
- E=none of these

GO ON TO THE NEXT COLUMN.———

GO ON TO THE NEXT PAGE.

95

In questions 101 through 105, compare the three names or numbers, and mark the answer

A   if ALL THREE names or numbers are exactly ALIKE
B   if only the FIRST and SECOND names or numbers are exactly ALIKE
C   if only the FIRST and THIRD names or numbers are exactly ALIKE
D   if only the SECOND and THIRD names or numbers are exactly ALIKE
E   if ALL THREE names or numbers are DIFFERENT

101. 1592514	1592574	1592574
102. 2010202	2010202	2010220
103. 6177396	6177936	6177396
104. Drusilla S. Ridgeley	Drusilla S. Ridgeley	Drusilla S. Ridgeley
105. Andrei I. Toumantzev	Andrei I. Tourmantzev	Andrei I. Toumantzov

In questions 106 through 110, find the correct place for the name in the box.

106. **Fitzsimmons, Hugh**
A)→
Fitts, Harold
B)→
Fitzgerald, June
C)→
FitzGibbon, Junius
D)→
FitzSimons, Martin
E)→

107. **D'Amato, Vincent**
A)→
Daly, Steven
B)→
D'Amboise, S. Vincent
C)→
Daniel, Vail
D)→
DeAlba, Valentina
E)→

108. **Schaeffer, Roger D.**
A)→
Schaffert, Evelyn M.
B)→
Schaffner, Margaret M.
C)→
Schafhirt, Milton G.
D)→
Shafer, Richard E.
E)→

109. **White-Lewis, Cecil**
A)→
Whitelaw, Cordelia
B)→
White-Leigh, Nancy
C)→
Whitely, Rodney
D)→
Whitlock, Warren
E)→

110. **VanDerHeggen, Don**
A)→
VanDemark, Doris
B)→
Vandenberg, H. E.
C)→
VanDercook, Marie
D)→
vanderLinden, Robert
E)→

GO ON TO THE NEXT COLUMN.

Answers

111. Add:
   7 5
+ 4 9
   —
A) 124   B) 125
C) 134   D) 225
E) none of these

112. Subtract:
   6 9
− 4 5
   —
A) 14   B) 23
C) 24   D) 26
E) none of these

113. Multiply:
   3 6
×   8
   —
A) 246   B) 262
C) 288   D) 368
E) none of these

114. Divide:
8 / 3 2 8
A) 31   B) 41
C) 42   D) 48
E) none of these

115. Multiply:
   5 8
×   9
   —
A) 472   B) 513
C) 521   D) 522
E) none of these

For each question below, find which one of the suggested answers appears in that question.

116.   Z 3 N P G 5 4 2

117.   6 N 2 8 G 4 P T

118.   6 N 4 T V G 8 2

119.   T 3 P 4 N 8 G 2

120.   6 7 K G N 2 L 5

Suggested Answers
A = 2, 3, G, N
B = 2, 6, N, T
C = 3, 4, G, K
D = 4, 6, K, T
E = none of these

KEY (CORRECT ANSWERS)

1. B	21. A	41. A	61. C	81. D	101. D
2. E	22. E	42. A	62. B	82. C	102. B
3. D	23. E	43. B	63. E	83. A	103. C
4. A	24. D	44. E	64. E	84. D	104. A
5. E	25. C	45. A	65. C	85. B	105. E
6. E	26. D	46. C	66. A	86. A	106. D
7. A	27. D	47. A	67. D	87. E	107. B
8. D	28. C	48. D	68. C	88. C	108. A
9. B	29. C	49. B	69. D	89. C	109. C
10. E	30. D	50. C	70. E	90. B	110. D
11. D	31. E	51. B	71. A	91. E	111. A
12. B	32. A	52. C	72. C	92. E	112. C
13. B	33. A	53. D	73. B	93. C	113. C
14. B	34. C	54. D	74. C	94. C	114. B
15. B	35. C	55. E	75. A	95. A	115. D
16. A	36. E	56. E	76. D	96. D	116. A
17. D	37. A	57. B	77. D	97. C	117. B
18. E	38. C	58. E	78. A	98. E	118. B
19. B	39. C	59. D	79. E	99. B	119. A
20. A	40. D	60. C	80. C	100. B	120. E

CODING

An ingenious question-type called coding, involving elements of alphabetizing, filing, name and number comparison, and evaluative judgment and application, has currently won wide acceptance in testing circles for measuring clerical aptitude and general ability, particularly on the senior (middle) grades (levels).

While the directions for this question usually vary in detail, the candidate is generally asked to consider groups of names, codes, and numbers, and, then, according to a given plan, to arrange codes in alphabetic order; to arrange these in numerical sequence; to re-arrange columns of names and numbers in correct order; to espy errors in coding; to choose the correct coding arrangement in consonance with the given directions and examples, etc.

This question-type appears to have few paramaters in respect to form, substance, or degree of difficulty.

Accordingly, acquaintance with, and practice in, the coding question is recommended for the serious candidate.

EXAMINATION SECTION
TEST 1

DIRECTIONS:

CODE TABLE

Name of Applicant	H	A	N	G	S	B	R	U	K	E
Test Code	c	o	m	p	l	e	x	i	t	y
File Number	0	1	2	3	4	5	6	7	8	9

Assume that each of the above *capital letters* is the first letter of the Name of an Applicant, that the *small letter* directly beneath each capital letter is the Test Code for the Applicant, and that the *number* directly beneath each code letter is the File Number for the Applicant.

In each of the following questions, the test code letters and the file numbers in Columns 2 and 3 should correspond to the capital letters in Column 1. For each question, look at each column carefully and mark your answer as follows:

If there is an error only in Column 2, mark your answer A.
If there is an error only in Column 3, mark your answer B.
If there is an error in both Columns 2 and 3, mark your answer C.
If both Columns 2 and 3 are correct, mark your answer D.

The following sample question is given to help you understand the procedure.

SAMPLE QUESTION

Column 1	Column 2	Column 3
AKEHN	otyci	18902

In Column 2, the final test code letter "i" should be "m." Column 3 is correctly coded to Column 1. Since there is an error only in Column 2, the answer is A

	Column 1	Column 2	Column 3	
1.	NEKKU	mytti	29987	1.
2.	KRAEB	txlye	86095	2.
3.	ENAUK	ymoit	92178	3.
4.	REANA	xeomo	69121	4.
5.	EKHSE	ytcxy	97049	5.

———

KEY (CORRECT ANSWERS)

1. B
2. C
3. D
4. A
5. C

———

TEST 2

DIRECTIONS: The employee identification codes in Column I begin and end with a capital letter and have an eight-digit number in between. In Questions 1 through 8,
employee identification codes in Column I are to be arranged according to the
following rules:

First: Arrange in alphabetical order according to the first letter.

Second: When two or more employee identification codes have the same first letter,
arrange in alphabetical order according to the last letter.

Third: When two or more employee codes have the same first and last letters,
arrange in numerical order beginning with the lowest number.

The employee identification codes in Column I are numbered 1 through 5 in the order in which
they are listed. In Column II the numbers 1 through 5 are arranged in four different ways to show
different arrangements of the corresponding employee identification numbers. Choose the
answer in Column II in which the employee identification numbers are arranged according to the
above rules.

SAMPLE QUESTION

Column I	Column II
1. E75044127B	A. 4, 1, 3, 2, 5
2. B96399104A	B. 4, 1, 2, 3, 5
3. B93939086A	C. 4, 3, 2, 5, 1
4. B47064465H	D. 3, 2, 5, 4, 1
5. B99040922A	

In the sample question, the four employee identification codes starting with B should be put
before the employee identification code starting with E. The employee identification codes starting with B and ending with A should be put before the employee identification codes starting
with B and ending with H. The three employee identification codes starting with B and ending
with A should be listed in numerical order, beginning with the lowest number. The correct way to
arrange the employee identification codes, therefore, is 3, 2, 5, 4, 1 shown below.

3.   B93939086A
2.   B96399104A
5.   B99040922A
4.   B47064465H
1.   E75044127B

Therefore, the answer to the sample question is D. Now answer the following questions according to the above rules.

Column I	Column II	
1. 1. G42786441J	A. 2, 5, 4, 3, 1	1.____
2. H45665413J	B. 5, 4, 1, 3, 2	
3. G43117690J	C. 4, 5, 1, 3, 2	
4. G435466981	D. 1, 3, 5, 4, 2	
5. G416799421		

2.
   1. S44556178T
   2. T43457169T
   3. S53321176T
   4. T53317998S
   5. S67673942S

   A. 1, 3, 5, 2, 4
   B. 4, 3, 5, 2, 1
   C. 5, 3, 1, 2, 4
   D. 5, 1, 3, 4, 2

3.
   1. R63394217D
   2. R63931247D
   3. R53931247D
   4. R66874239D
   4. R46799366D

   A. 5, 4, 2, 3, 1
   B. 1, 5, 3, 2, 4
   C. 5, 3, 1, 2, 4
   D. 5, 1, 2, 3, 4

4.
   1. A35671968B
   2. A35421794C
   3. A35466987B
   4. C10435779A
   5. C00634779B

   A. 3, 2, 1, 4, 5
   B. 2, 3, 1, 5, 4
   C. 1, 3, 2, 4, 5
   D. 3, 1, 2, 4, 5

5.
   1. I99746426Q
   2. I10445311Q
   3. J63749877P
   4. J03421739Q
   5. J00765311Q

   A. 2, 1, 3, 5, 4
   B. 5, 4, 2, 1, 3
   C. 4, 5, 3, 2, 1
   D. 2, 1, 4, 5, 3

6.
   1. M33964217N
   2. N33942770N
   3. N06155881M
   4. M00433669M
   5. M79034577N

   A. 4, 1, 5, 2, 3
   B. 5, 1, 4, 3, 2
   C. 4, 1, 5, 3, 2
   D. 1, 4, 5, 2, 3

7.
   1. D77643905C
   2. D44106788C
   3. D13976022F
   4. D97655430E
   5. D00439776F

   A. 1, 2, 5, 3, 4
   B. 5, 3, 2, 1, 4
   C. 2, 1, 5, 3, 4
   D. 2, 1, 4, 5, 3

8.
   1. W22746920A
   2. W22743720A
   3. W32987655A
   4. W43298765A
   5. W30987433A

   A. 2, 1, 3, 4, 5
   B. 2, 1, 5, 3, 4
   C. 1, 2, 3, 4, 5
   D. 1, 2, 5, 3, 4

2
3
4
5
6
7
8.

KEY (CORRECT ANSWERS)

1.	B	5.	A
2.	D	6.	C
3.	C	7.	D
4.	D	8.	B

TEST 3

DIRECTIONS: Each of the following equestions consists of three sets of names and name codes. In each question, the two names and name codes on the same line are supposed to be exactly the same.

Look carefully at each set of names and codes and mark your answer:
- A. if there are mistakes in all three sets
- B. if there are mistakes in two of the sets
- C. if there is a mistake in only one set
- D. if there are no mistakes in any of the sets

The following sample question is given to help you understand the procedure.

Macabe, John N. - V 53162	Macade, John N. - V 53162	
Howard, Joan S. - J 24791	Howard, Joan S. - J 24791	
Ware, Susan B. - A 45068	Ware, Susan B. - A 45968	

In the above sample question, the names and name codes of the first set are not exactly the same because of the spelling of the last name (Macabe - Macade). The names and name codes of the second set are exactly the same. The names and name codes of the third set are not exactly the same because the two name codes are different (A 45068 - A 45968), Since there are mistakes in only 2 of the sets, the answer to the sample question is B.

1. Powell, Michael C. - 78537 F   Powell, Michael C. - 78537 F   1.____
    Martinez, Pablo, J. - 24435 P   Martinez, Pablo J. - 24435 P
    MacBane, Eliot M. - 98674 E   MacBane, Eliot M. - 98674 E

2. Fitz-Kramer Machines Inc. - 259090   Fitz-Kramer Machines Inc. - 259090   2.____
    Marvel Cleaning Service - 482657   Marvel Cleaning Service - 482657
    Donate, Carl G. - 637418   Danato, Carl G. - 687418

3. Martin Davison Trading Corp. - 43108 T Martin Davidson Trading Corp. - 43108 T 3.____
    Cotwald Lighting Fixtures - 76065 L   Cotwald Lighting Fixtures - 70056 L
    R. Crawford Plumbers - 23157 C   R. Crawford Plumbers - 23157 G

4. Fraiman Engineering Corp. - M4773   Friaman Engineering Corp. -M4773   4.____
    Neuman, Walter B. - N7745   Neumen, Walter B. - N7745
    Pierce, Eric M. - W6304   Pierce, Eric M. - W6304

5. Constable, Eugene - B 64837   Comstable, Eugene - B 64837   5.____
    Derrick, Paul - H 27119   Derrik, Paul - H 27119
    Heller, Karen - S 49606   Heller, Karen - S 46906

6. Hernando Delivery Service Co. - D 7456 Hernando Delivery Service Co. - D 7456 6.____
    Barettz Electrical Supplies - N 5392   Barettz Electrical Supplies - N 5392
    Tanner, Abraham - M 4798   Tanner, Abraham - M 4798

7. Kalin Associates - R 38641   Kaline Associates - R 38641   7.____
    Sealey, Robert E. - P 63533   Sealey, Robert E. - P 63553
    Scalsi Office Furniture   Scalsi Office Furniture

8. Janowsky, Philip M.- 742213
    Hansen, Thomas H. - 934816
    L. Lester and Son Inc. - 294568

Janowsky, Philip M.- 742213
Hanson, Thomas H. - 934816
L. Lester and Son Inc. - 294568

8.__

KEY (CORRECT ANSWERS)

1. D
2. C
3. A
4. B
5. A

6. D
7. B
8. C

TEST 4

DIRECTIONS: The following questions are to be answered on the basis of the following Code Table. In this table, for each number, a corresponding code letter is given. Each of the questions contains three pairs of numbers and code letters. In each pair, the code letters should correspond with the numbers in accordance with the Code Table.

CODE TABLE

Number	1	2	3	4	5	6	7	8	9	0
Corresponding Code Letter	Y	N	Z	X	W	T	U	P	S	R

In some of the pairs below, an error exists in the coding. Examine the pairs in each question carefully. If an error exists in:

Only one of the pairs in the question, mark your answer A.
Any two pairs in the question, mark your answer B.
All three pairs in the question, mark your answer C.
None of the pairs in the question, mark your answer D.

SAMPLE QUESTION

37258   -   ZUNWP
948764   -   SXPTTX
73196   -   UZYSP

In the above sample, the first pair is correct since each number, as listed, has the correct corresponding code letter. In the second pair, an error exists because the number 7 should have the code letter U instead of the letter T. In the third pair, an error exists because the number 6 should have the code letter T instead of the letter P. Since there are errors in two of the three pairs, the correct answer is B.

1. 493785   -   XSZUPW   1._____
   86398207   -   PTUSPNRU
   5943162   -   WSXZYTN

2. 5413968412   -   WXYZSTPXYR   2._____
   8763451297   -   PUTZXWYZSU
   4781965302   -   XUPYSUWZRN

3. 79137584   -   USYRUWPX   3._____
   638247   -   TZPNXS
   49679312   -   XSTUSZYN

4. 37854296   -   ZUPWXNST   4._____
   09183298   -   RSYXZNSP
   91762358   -   SYUTNXWP

5. 3918762485   -   ZSYPUTNXPW   5._____
   1578291436   -   YWUPNSYXZT
   2791385674   -   NUSYZPWTUX

6. 197546821   - YSUWSTPNY
     873024867   - PUZRNWPTU
     583179246   - WPZYURNXT

7. 510782463   - WYRUSNXTZ
     478192356   - XUPYSNZWT
     961728532   - STYUNPWXN

6.

7.

KEY (CORRECT ANSWERS)

1. A
2. C
3. B
4. B
5. D

6. C
7. B

TEST 5

DIRECTIONS: Assume that each of the capital letters is the first letter of the name of a city using EAM equipment. The number directly beneath each capital letter is the code number for the city. The small letter beneath each code number is the code letter for the number of EAM divisions in the city and the + or - symbol directly beneath each code letter is the code symbol which signifies whether or not the city uses third generation computers with the EAM equipment.

The questions that follow show City Letters in Column I, Code Numbers in Column II, Code Letters in Column III, and Code Symbols in Column IV. If correct. each Citv Letter in Column I should correspond by position with each of the three codes shown in the other three columns, in accordance with the coding key shown. *BUT* there are some errors. For each question,

> If there is a total of *ONE* error in Columns 2, 3, and 4, mark your answer A.
> If there is a total of *TWO* errors in Columns 2, 3, and 4, mark your answer B.
> If there is a total of *THREE* errors in Columns 2, 3, and 4, mark your answer C.
> If Columns 2, 3, and 4 are correct, mark your answer D.

SAMPLE QUESTION

I City Letter	II Code Numbers	III Code Letters	IV Code Symbols
Y J M O S	5 3 7 9 8	e b g i h	- - + + -

The errors are as follows: In Column 2, the Code Number should be "2" instead of "3" for City Letter "J," and in Column 4 the Code Symbol should be "+" instead of "-" for City Letter "Y." Since there is a total of two errors in Columns 2, 3, and 4, the answer to this sample question is B.

Now answer questions 1 through 9 according to these rules.

CODING KEY

City Letter		P	J	R	T	Y	K	M	S	0
Code Number		1	2	3	4	5	6	7	8	9
Code Letter		a	b	c	d	e	f	g	h	i
Code Symbol		+	-	+	-	+	-	+	-	+

	I City Letters	II Code Numbers	III Code Letters	IV Code Symbols	
1.	K O R M P	6 9 3 7 1	f i e g a	- - + + +	1._____
2.	O T P S Y	9 4 1 8 6	b d a h e	+ - - - +	2._____
3.	R S J T M	3 8 1 4 7	c h b e g	- - - - +	3._____
4.	P M S K J	1 7 8 6 2	a g h f b	+ + - - -	4._____
5.	M Y T J R	7 5 4 2 3	g e d f c	+ + - - +	5._____
6.	T P K Y O	4 1 6 7 9	d a f e i	- + - + -	6._____
7.	S K O R T	8 6 9 3 5	h f i c d	- - + + -	7._____
8.	J R Y P K	2 3 5 1 9	b d e a f	- + + + -	8._____
9.	R O M P Y	4 9 7 1 5	c i g a d	+ + - + +	9._____

KEY (CORRECT ANSWERS)

1. B
2. C
3. C
4. D
5. A

6. B
7. A
8. B
9. C

———————

TEST 6

Assume that each of the capital letters is the first letter of the name of an offense, that the small letter directly beneath each capital letter is the code letter for the offense, and that the number directly beneath each code letter is the file number for the offense.

DIRECTIONS: In each of the following questions, the code letters and file numbers should correspond to the capital letters.

If there is an error only in Column 2, mark your answer A.
If there is an error only in Column 3, mark your answer B.
If there is an error in both Column 2 and Column 3, mark your answer C.
If both Columns 2 and 3 are correct, mark your answer D.

SAMPLE QUESTION

Column 1	Column 2	Column 3
BNARGHSVVU	emoxtylcci	6357905118

The code letters in Column 2 are correct but the first "5" in Column 3 should be "2." Therefore, the answer is B. Now answer the following questions according to the above rules.

CODE TABLE

Name of Offense	V A N D S B R U G H
Code Letter	c o m p l e x i t y
File Number	1 2 3 4 5 6 7 8 9 0

	Column 1	Column 2	Column 3	
1.	HGDSBNBSVR	ytplxmelcx	0945736517	1._____
2.	SDGUUNHVAH	lptiimycoy	5498830120	2._____
3.	BRSNAAVUDU	exlmooctpi	6753221848	3._____
4.	VSRUDNADUS	cleipmopil	1568432485	4._____
5.	NDSHVRBUAG	mplycxeiot	3450175829	5._____
6.	GHUSNVBRDA	tyilmcexpo	9085316742	6._____
7.	DBSHVURANG	pesycixomt	4650187239	7._____
8.	RHNNASBDGU	xymnolepti	7033256398	8._____

KEY (CORRECT ANSWERS)

1. C
2. D
3. A
4. C
5. B

6. D
7. A
8. C

TEST 7

DIRECTIONS: Each of the following questions contains three sets of code letters and code numbers. In each set, the code numbers should correspond with the code letters as given in the Table, but there is a coding error in some of the sets. Examine the sets in each question carefully.

Mark your answer A if there is a coding error in only *ONE* of the sets in the question.
Mark your answer B if there is a coding error in any *TWO* of the sets in the question.
Mark your answer C if there is a coding error in all *THREE* sets in the question.
Mark your answer D if there is a coding error in *NONE* of the sets in the question.

SAMPLE QUESTION

fgzduwaf	-	35720843
uabsdgfw	-	04262538
hhfaudgs	-	99340257

In the above sample question, the first set is right because each code number matches the code letter as in the Code Table. In the second set, the corresponding number for the code letter b is wrong because it should be 1 instead of 2. In the third set, the corresponding number for the last code letter s is wrong because it should be 6 instead of 7. Since there is an error in two of the sets, the answer to the above sample question is B.

In the Code Table below, each code letter has a corresponding code number directly beneath it.

CODE TABLE

Code Letter	b	d	f	a	g	s	z	w	h	u
Code Number	1	2	3	4	5	6	7	8	9	0

1. fsbughwz - 36104987   zwubgasz - 78025467   1.____
   ghgufddb - 59583221

2. hafgdaas - 94351446   ddsfabsd - 22734162   2.____
   wgdbssgf - 85216553

3. abfbssbd - 41316712   ghzfaubs - 59734017   3.____
   sdbzfwza - 62173874

4. whfbdzag - 89412745   daaszuub - 24467001   4.____
   uzhfwssd - 07936623

5. zbadgbuh - 71425109   dzadbbsz - 27421167   5.____
   gazhwaff - 54798433

6. fbfuadsh - 31304265   gzfuwzsb - 57300671   6.____
   bashhgag - 14699535

KEY (CORRECT ANSWERS)

1. B
2. C
3. B
4. B
5. D
6. C

———

TEST 8

DIRECTIONS: The following questions are to be answered on the basis of the following Code Table. In this table every letter has a corresponding code number to be punched. Each question contains three pairs of letters and code numbers. In each pair, the code numbers should correspond with the letters in accordance with the Code Table.

CODE TABLE

Letter	P	L	A	N	D	C	0	B	U	R
Corresponding Code Number	1	2	3	4	5	6	7	8	9	0

In some of the pairs below, an error exists in the coding. Examine the pairs in each question. Mark your answer

A if there is a mistake in only *one* of the pairs
B if there is a mistake in only *two* of the pairs
C if there is a mistake in *all three* of the pairs
D if there is a mistake in *none* of the pairs

SAMPLE QUESTION

LCBPUPAB - 26819138
ACOABOL - 3683872
NDURONUC - 46901496

In the above sample, the first pair is correct since each letter as listed has the correct corresponding code number. In the second pair, an error exists because the letter 0 should have the code number 7, instead of 8. In the third pair, an error exists because the letter D should have the code number 5, instead of 6. Since there are errors in two of the three pairs, your answer should be B.

1. ADCANPLC - 35635126   DORURBBO - 57090877   1.____
   PNACBUCP - 14368061

2. LCOBLRAP - 26782931   UPANUPCD - 91349156   2.____
   RLDACLRO - 02536207

3. LCOROPAR - 26707130   BALANRUP - 83234091   3.____
   DOPOAULL - 57173922

4. ONCRUBAP - 74609831   DCLANORD - 56243705   4.____
   AORPDUR - 3771590

5. PANRBUCD - 13408965   UAOCDPLR - 93765120   5.____
   OPDDOBRA - 71556803

6. BAROLDCP - 83072561   PNOCOBLA - 14767823   6.____
   BURPDOLA - 89015723

7. ANNCPABO - 34461387   DBALDRCP - 58325061   7.____
   ACRPOUL - 3601792

113

8. BLAPOUR - 8321790   NOACNPL - 4736412   8.__
    RODACORD - 07536805

9. ADUBURCL- 3598062   NOCOBAPR - 47578310   9.__
    PRONDALU - 10754329

10. UBADCLOR - 98356270   NBUPPARA - 48911033   10.__
    LONDUPRC - 27459106

KEY (CORRECT ANSWERS)

1. C
2. B
3. D
4. B
5. A

6. D
7. B
8. B
9. C
10. A

TEST 9

DIRECTIONS: Answer questions 1 through 10 ONLY on the basis of the following information.

Column I consists of serial numbers of dollar bills. Column II shows different ways of arranging the corresponding serial numbers.

The serial numbers of dollar bills in Column I begin and end with a capital letter and have an eight-digit number in between. The serial numbers in Column I are to be arranged according to the following rules:

FIRST: In alphabetical order according to the first letter.

SECOND: When two or more serial numbers have the same first letter, in alphabetical order according to the last letter.

THIRD: When two or more serial numbers have the same first and last letters, in numerical order, beginning with the lowest number.

The serial numbers in Column I are numbered (1) through (5) in the order in which they are listed. In Column II the numbers (1) through (5) are arranged in four different ways to show different arrangements of the corresponding serial numbers. Choose the answer in Column II in which the serial numbers are arranged according to the above rules.

SAMPLE QUESTION

	COLUMN I		COLUMN II
(1)	E75044127B	(A)	4, 1, 3, 2, 5
(2)	B96399104A	(B)	4, 1, 2, 3, 5
(3)	B93939086A	(C)	4, 3, 2, 5, 1
(4)	B47064465H	(D)	3, 2, 5, 4, 1
(5)	B99040922A		

In the sample question, the four serial numbers starting with B should be put before the serial number starting with E. The serial numbers starting with B and ending with A should be put before the serial number starting with B and ending with H. The three serial numbers starting with B and ending with A should be listed in numerical order, beginning with the lowest number. The correct way to arrange the serial numbers, therefore, is:

(3)	B93939086A
(2)	B96399104A
(5)	B99040922A
(4)	B47064465H
(1)	E75044127B

Since the order of arrangement is 3, 2, 5, 4, 1, the answer to the sample question is (D).

	COLUMN I		COLUMN II
1. (1)	P44343314Y	A.	2, 3, 1, 4, 5
(2)	P44141341S	B.	1, 5, 3, 2, 4
(3)	P44141431L	C.	4, 2, 3, 5, 1
(4)	P41143413W	D.	5, 3, 2, 4, 1
(5)	P44313433H		
2. (1)	D89077275M	A.	3, 2, 5, 4, 1
(2)	D98073724N	B.	1, 4, 3, 2, 5
(3)	D90877274N	C.	4, 1, 5, 2, 3
(4)	D98877275M	D.	1, 3, 2, 5, 4
(5)	D98873725N		

3.	(1)	H32548137E	A.	2,	4,	5,	1,	3
	(2)	H35243178A	B.	1,	5,	2,	3,	4
	(3)	H35284378F	C.	1,	5,	2,	4,	3
	(4)	H35288337A	D.	2,	1,	5,	3,	4
	(5)	H32883173B						
4.	(1)	K24165039H	A.	4,	2,	5,	3,	1
	(2)	F24106599A	B.	2,	3,	4,	1,	5
	(3)	L21406639G	C.	4,	2,	5,	1,	3
	(4)	C24156093A	D.	1,	3,	4,	5,	2
	(5)	K24165593D						
5.	(1)	H79110642E	A.	2,	1,	3,	5,	4
	(2)	H79101928E	B.	2,	1,	4,	5,	3
	(3)	A79111567F	C.	3,	5,	2,	1,	4
	(4)	H79111796E	D.	4,	3,	5,	1,	2
	(5)	A79111618F						
6.	(1)	P16388385W	A.	3,	4,	5,	2,	1
	(2)	R16388335V	B.	2,	3,	4,	5,	1
	(3)	P16383835W	C.	2,	4,	3,	1,	5
	(4)	R18386865V	D.	3,	1,	5,	2,	4
	(5)	P18686865W						
7.	(1)	B42271749G	A.	4,	1,	5,	2,	3
	(2)	B42271779G	B.	4,	1,	2,	5,	3
	(3)	E43217779G	C.	1,	2,	4,	5,	3
	(4)	B42874119C	D.	5,	3,	1,	2,	4
	(5)	E42817749G						
8.	(1)	M57906455S	A.	4,	1,	5,	3,	2
	(2)	N87077758S	B.	3,	4,	1,	5,	2
	(3)	N87707757B	C.	4,	1,	5,	2,	3
	(4)	M57877759B	D.	1,	5,	3,	2,	4
	(5)	M57906555S						
9.	(1)	C69336894Y	A.	2,	5,	3,	1,	4
	(2)	C69336684V	B.	3,	2,	5,	1,	4
	(3)	C69366887W	C.	3,	1,	4,	5,	2
	(4)	C69366994Y	D.	2,	5,	1,	3,	4
	(5)	C69336865V						
10.	(1)	A56247181D	A.	1,	5,	3,	2,	4
	(2)	A56272128P	B.	3,	1,	5,	2,	4
	(3)	H56247128D	C.	3,	2,	1,	5,	4
	(4)	H56272288P	D.	1,	5,	2,	3,	4
	(5)	A56247188D						

KEY (CORRECT ANSWERS)

1.	D		6.	D
2.	B		7.	B
3.	A		8.	A
4.	C		9.	A
5.	C		10.	D

TEST 10

DIRECTIONS: Answer the following questions on the basis of the instructions, the code, and the sample questions given below. Assume that an officer at a certain location is equipped with a two-way radio to keep him in constant touch with his security headquarters. Radio messages and replies are given in code form, as follows:

CODE TABLE

Radio Code for Situation	J	P	M	F	B
Radio Code for Action to be Taken	o	r	a	z	q
Radio Response for Action Being Taken	1	2	3	4	5

Assume that each of the above capital letters is the radio code for a particular type of situation, that the small letter below each capital letter is the radio code for the action an officer is directed to take, and that the number directly below each small letter is the radio response an officer should make to indicate what action was actually taken.

In each of the following questions, the code letter for the action directed (Column 2) and the code number for the action taken (Column 3) should correspond to the capital letters in Column 1.

INSTRUCTIONS: If only Column 2 is different from Column 1, mark your answer I.
If only Column 3 is different from Column 1, mark your answer II.
If both Column 2 and Column 3 are different from Column I, mark your answer III.
If both Columns 2 and 3 are the same as Column 1, mark your answer IV.

SAMPLE QUESTION

Column 1	Column 2	Column 3
JPFMB	orzaq	12453

The CORRECT answer is: A. I B. II C. III D. IV
The code letters in Column 2 are correct, but the numbers "53" in Column 3 should be "35." Therefore, the answer is B. Now answe the following questions according to the above rules.

Column 1	Column 2	Column 3	
1. PBFJM	rqzoa	25413	1._____
2. MPFBJ	zrqao	32541	2._____
3. JBFPM	oqzra	15432	3._____
4. BJPMF	qaroz	51234	4._____
5. PJFMB	rozaq	21435	5._____
6. FJBMP	zoqra	41532	6._____

KEY (CORRECT ANSWERS)

1. D
2. C
3. B
4. A
5. D
6. A

———

BASIC FUNDAMENTALS OF FILING SCIENCE

TABLE OF CONTENTS

Page

I. COMMENTARY 1

II. BASIS OF FILING 1
  1. Types of Files 1
    (1) Shannon File 1
    (2) Spindle File 1
    (3) Box File 1
    (4) Flat File 1
    (5) Bellows File 1
    (6) Vertical File 1
    (7) Clip File 1
    (8) Visible File 1
    (9) Rotary File 1
  2. Aids in Filing 2
  3. Variations of Filing Systems 2
  4. Centralized Filing 2
  5. Methods of Filing 2
    (1) Alphabetic Filing 3
    (2) Subject Filing 3
    (3) Geographical File 3
    (4) Chronological File 3
    (5) Numerical File 3
  6. Indexing 3
  7. Alphabetizing 3

III. RULES FOR INDEXING AND ALPHABETIZING 3

IV. OFFICIAL EXAMINATION DIRECTIONS AND RULES 7
  Official Directions 8
  Official Rules for Alphabetical Filing 8
    Names of Individuals 8
    Names of Business Organizations 8
  Sample Question 8

BASIC FUNDAMENTALS OF FILING SCIENCE

I. COMMENTARY

Filing is the systematic arrangement and storage of papers, cards, forms, catalogues, etc., so that they may be found easily and quickly. The importance of an efficient filing system cannot be emphasized too strongly. The filed materials form records which may be needed quickly to settle questions that may cause embarrassing situations if such evidence is not available. In addition to keeping papers in order so that they are readily available, the filing system must also be designed to keep papers in good condition. A filing system must be planned so that papers may be filed easily, withdrawn easily, and as quickly returned to their proper place. The cost of a filing system is also an important factor.

The need for a filing system arose when the business man began to carry on negotiations on a large scale. He could no longer be intimate with the details of his business. What was needed in the early era was a spindle or pigeon-hole desk. Filing in pigeon-hole desks is now almost completely extinct. It was an unsatisfactory practice since pigeon holes were not labeled, and the desk was an untidy mess.

II. BASIS OF FILING

The science of filing is an exact one and entails a thorough understanding of basic facts, materials, and methods. An overview of this important information now follows.

1. Types of files

(1) SHANNON FILE

This consists of a board, at one end of which are fastened two arches which may be opened laterally.

(2) SPINDLE FILE

This consists of a metal or wood base to which is attached a long, pointed spike. Papers are pushed down on the spike as received. This file is useful for temporary retention of papers.

(3) BOX FILE

This is a heavy cardboard or metal box, opening from the side like a book.

(4) FLAT FILE

This consists of a series of shallow drawers or trays, arranged like drawers in a cabinet.

(5) BELLOWS FILE

This is a heavy cardboard container with alphabetized or compartment sections, the ends of which are closed in such a manner that they resemble an accordion.

(6) VERTICAL FILE

This consists of one or more drawers in which the papers are stood on edge, usually in folders, and are indexed by guides. A series of two or more drawers in one unit is the usual file cabinet.

(7) CLIP FILE

This file has a large clip attached to a board and is very similar to the *SHANNON FILE.*

(8) VISIBLE FILE

Cards are filed flat in an overlapping arrangement which leaves a part of each card visible at all times.

(9) ROTARY FILE

The *ROTARY FILE* has a number of visible card files attached to a post around which they can be revolved. The wheel file has visible cards which rotate around a horizontal axle.

(10) TICKLER FILE

This consists of cards or folders marked with the days of the month, in which materials are filed and turned up on the appropriate day of the month.

2. Aids in filing

(1) GUIDES

Guides are heavy cardboard, pasteboard, or bristol-board sheets the same size as folders. At the top is a tab on which is marked or printed the distinguishing letter, words, or numbers indicating the material filed in a section of the drawer.

(2) SORTING TRAYS

Sorting trays are equipped with alphabetical guides to facilitate the sorting of papers preparatory to placing them in a file.

(3) CODING

Once the classification or indexing caption has been determined, it must be indicated on the letter for filing purposes.

(4) CROSS REFERENCE

Some letters or papers might easily be called for under two or more captions. For this purpose, a cross-reference card or sheet is placed in the folder or in the index.

3. Variations of filing systems

(1) VARIADEX ALPHABETIC INDEX

Provides for more effective expansion of the alphabetic system.

(2) TRIPLE-CHECK NUMERIC FILING

Entails a multiple cross-reference, as the name implies.

(3) VARIADEX FILING

Makes use of color as an aid in filing.

(4) DEWEY DECIMAL SYSTEM

The system is a numeric one used in libraries or for filing library materials in an office. This special type of filing system is used where material is grouped in finely divided categories, such as in libraries. With this method, all material to be filed is divided into ten major groups, from 000 to 900, and then subdivided into tens, units, and decimals.

4. Centralized filing

Centralized filing means keeping the files in one specific or central location. Decentralized filing means putting away papers in files of individual departments. The first step in the organization of a central filing department is to make a careful canvass of all desks in the offices. In this manner we can determine just what material needs to be filed, and what information each desk occupant requires from the central file. Only papers which may be used at some time by persons in the various offices should be placed in the central file. A paper that is to be used at some time by persons in the various offices should be placed in the central file. A paper that is to be used by one department only should never be filed in the central file.

5. Methods of filing

While there are various methods used for filing, actually there are only five basic systems: alphabetical, subject, numerical, geographic, and chronological. All other systems are derived from one of these or from a combination of two or more of them.

Since the purpose of a filing system is to store business records <u>systemically</u> so that any particular record can be found almost instantly when required, filing requires, in addition to the proper kinds of equipment and supplies, an effective method of indexing.

There are five basic systems of filing:

(1) ALPHABETIC FILING

Most filing is alphabetical. Other methods, as described below, require extensive alphabetization.

In alphabetic filing, lettered dividers or guides are arranged in alphabetic sequence. Material to be filed is placed behind the proper guide. All materials under each letter are also arranged alphabetically. Folders are used unless the file is a card index.

(2) SUBJECT FILING

This method is used when a single, complete file on a certain subject is desired. A subject file is often maintained to assemble all correspondence on a certain subject. Such files are valuable in connection with insurance claims, contract negotiations, personnel, and other investigations, special programs, and similar subjects.

(3) GEOGRAPHICAL FILE

Materials are filed according to location: states, cities, counties, or other subdivisions. Statistics and tax information are often filed in this manner.

(4) CHRONOLOGICAL FILE

Records are filed according to date. This method is used especially in "tickler" files that have guides numbered 1 to 31 for each day of the month. Each number indicates the day of the month when the filed item requires attention.

(5) NUMERICAL FILE

This method requires an alphabetic card index giving name and number. The card index is used to locate records numbered consecutively in the files according to date received or sequence in which issued, such as licenses, permits, etc.

6. <u>Indexing</u>

Determining the name or title under which an item is to be filed is known as <u>indexing</u>. For example, how would a letter from Robert E. Smith be filed? The name would be rearranged Smith,Robert E., so that the letter would be filed under the last name.

7. <u>Alphabetizing</u>

The arranging of names for filing is known as <u>alphabetizing</u>. For example, suppose you have four letters indexed under the names Johnson, Becker, Roe, and Stern. How should these letters be arranged in the files so that they may be found easily? You would arrange the four names alphabetically, thus, Becker, Johnson, Roe, and Stern.

III. RULES FOR INDEXING AND ALPHABETIZING

1. The names of persons are to be transposed. Write the surname first, then the given name, and, finally, the middle name or initial. Then arrange the various names according to the alphabetic order of letters throughout the entire name. If there is a title, consider that after the middle name or initial.

NAMES	INDEXED AS
Arthur L.Bright	Bright, Arthur L.
Arthur S.Bright	Bright, Arthur S.
P.E. Cole	Cole, P.E.

| | Dr. John C. Fox | Fox, John C. (Dr.) |

2. If a surname includes the same letters of another surname, with one or more additional letters added to the end, the shorter surname is placed first regardless of the given name or the initial of the given name.

NAMES	INDEXED AS
Robert E. Brown	Brown, Robert E.
Gerald A. Browne	Browne, Gerald A.
William O. Brownell	Brownell, William O.

3. Firm names are alphabetized under the surnames. Words like the, an, a, of, and for, are not considered.

NAMES	INDEXED AS
Bank of America	Bank of America
Bank Discount Dept.	Bank Discount Dept.
The Cranford Press	Cranford Press, The
Nelson Dwyer & Co.	Dwyer, Nelson, & Co.
Sears, Roebuck & Co.	Sears, Roebuck & Co.
Montgomery Ward & Co.	Ward, Montgomery, & Co.

4. The order of filing is determined first of all by the first letter of the names to be filed. If the first letters are the same, the order is determined by the second letters, and so on. In the following pairs of names, the order is determined by the letters underlined:

Austen Hayes Hanson Harvey Heath Green Schwartz
Baker   Heath Harper Harwood Heaton Greene Schwarz

5. When surnames are alike, those with initials only precede those with given names, unless the first initial comes alphabetically after the first letter of the name.

Gleason, S.	but,	Abbott, Mary
Gleason, S.W.		Abbott, W.B.
Gleason, Sidney		

6. Hyphenated names are treated as if spelled without the hyphen.

| Lloyd, Paul N. | Lloyd, Robert |
| Lloyd-Jones, James | Lloyd-Thomas, A.S. |

7. Company names composed of single letters which are not used as abbreviations precede the other names beginning with the same letter.

B & S Garage	E Z Duplicator Co.
B X Cable Co.	Eagle Typewriter Co.
Babbitt, R.N.	Edison Company

8. The ampersand (&) and the apostrophe (') in firm names are disregarded in alphabetizing.

Nelson & Niller	M & C Amusement Corp.
Nelson, Walter J.	M C Art Assn.
Nelson's Bakery	

9. Names beginning with Mac, Mc, or M' are usually placed in regular order as spelled. Some filing systems file separately names beginning with Mc.

MacDonald, R.J.	Mazza, Anthony
Macdonald, S.B.	McAdam, Wm.
Mace, Wm.	McAndrews, Jerry

10. Names beginning with St. are listed as if the name Saint were spelled in full. Numbered street names and all abbreviated names are treated as if spelled out in full.

Saginaw	Fifth Avenue Hotel	Hart Mfg. Co.
St. Louis	42nd Street Dress Shop	Hart, Martin
St. Peter's Rectory	Hart, Chas.	Hart, Thos.

Sandford	Hart, Charlotte	Hart, Thomas A.
Smith, Wm.	Hart, Jas.	Hart, Thos. R.
Smith, Willis	Hart, Janice	

11. Federal, state, or city departments of government should be placed alphabetically under the governmental branch controlling them.

> Illinois, State of -- Departments and Commissions
> > Banking Dept.
> > Employment Bureau
> United States Government Departments
> > Commerce
> > Defense
> > State
> > Treasury

12. Alphabetic order

Each word in a name is an indexing unit. Arrange the names in alphabetic order by comparing similar units in each name. Consider the second units only when the first units are identical. Consider the third units only when both the first and second units are identical.

13. Single surnames or initials

A surname, when used alone, precedes the same surname with a first name or initial. A surname with a first initial only precedes a surname with a complete first name. This rule is sometimes stated, "nothing comes before something."

14. Surname prefixes

A surname prefix is not a separate indexing unit, but it is considered part of the surname. These prefixes include: d', D', Da, de, De, Del, Des, Di, Du, Fitz., La, Le, Mc, Mac, 'c, O', St., Van, Van der, Von, Von der, and others. The prefixes M', Mac, and Mc are indexed and filed exactly as they are spelled.

15. Names of firms

Names of firms and institutions are indexed and filed exactly as they are written when they do not contain the complete name of an individual.

16. Names of firms containing complete individual names

When the firm or institution name includes the complete name of an individual, the units are transposed for indexing in the same way as the name of an individual.

17. Article "The"

When the article the occurs at the beginning of a name, it is placed at the end in parentheses but it is not moved. In both cases, it is not an indexing unit and is disregarded in filing.

18. Hyphenated names

Hyphenated firm names are considered as separate indexing units. Hyphenated surnames of individuals are considered as one indexing unit; this applies also to hyphenated names of individuals whose complete names are part of a firm name.

19. Abbreviations

Abbreviations are considered as though the name were written in full; however, single letters other than abbreviations are considered as separate indexing units.

20. Conjunctions, prepositions and firm endings

Conjunctions and prepositions, such as and, for, in, of, are disregarded in indexing and filing but are not omitted or their order changed when writing names on cards and folders. Firm endings, such as Ltd., Inc., Co., Son, Bros., Mfg., and Corp., are treated as a unit in indexing and filing and are considered as though spelled in full, such as Brothers and Incorporated.

21. One or two words

    Names that may be spelled either as one or two words are indexed and filed as one word.

22. Compound geographic names

    Compound geographic names are considered as separate indexing and filing units, except when the first part of the name is not an English word, such as the Los in Los Angeles.

23. Titles or degrees of individuals, whether preceding or following the name, are not considered in indexing or filing. They are placed in parentheses after the given name or initial. Terms that designate seniority, such as Jr., Sr., 2d, are also placed in parentheses and are considered for indexing and filing only when the names to be indexed are otherwise identical.

    Exception A:

    When the name of an individual consists of a title and one name only, such as Queen Elizabeth, it is not transposed and the title is considered for indexing and filing.

    Exception B:

    When a title or foreign article is the initial word of a firm or association name, it is considered for indexing and filing.

24. Possessives

    When a word ends in apostrophe s, the s is not considered in indexing and filing. However, when a word ends in s apostrophe, because the s is part of the original word, it is considered. This rule is sometimes stated, "Consider everything up to the apostrophe. "

25. United States and foreign government names

    Names pertaining to the federal government are indexed and filed under United States Government and then subdivided by title of the department, bureau, division, commission, or board. Names pertaining to foreign governments are indexed and filed under names of countries and then subdivided by title of the department, bureau, division, commission, or board. Phrases, such as department of, bureau of, division of, commission of, board of, when used in titles of governmental bodies, are placed in parentheses after the word they modify, but are disregarded in indexing and filing. Such phrases, however, are considered in indexing and filing nongovernmental names.

26. Other political subdivisions

    Names pertaining to other political subdivisions, such as states, counties, cities, or towns, are indexed and filed under the name of the political subdivision and then subdivided by the title of the department, bureau, division, commission, or board.

27. Addresses

    When the same name appears with different addresses, the names are indexed as usual and arranged alphabetically according to city or town. The State is considered only when there is duplication of both individual or company name and city name. If the same name is located at different addresses within the same city, then the names are arranged alphabetically by streets. If the same name is located at more than one address on the same street, then the names are arranged from the lower to the higher street number.

28. Numbers

    Any number in a name is considered as though it were written in words, and it is indexed and filed as one unit.

29. Bank names

   Because the names of many banking institutions are alike in several respects, as first National Bank, Second National Bank, etc., banks are indexed and filed first by city location, then by bank name, with the state location written in parentheses and considered only if necessary

30. Married women

   The legal name of a married woman is the one used for filing purposes. Legally, a man's surname is the only part of a man's name a woman assumes when she marries. Her legal name, therefore, could be either:

   (1) Her own first and middle names together with her husband's surname, or
   (2) Her own first name and maiden surname, together with her husband's surname.

   Mrs. is placed in parentheses at the end of the name. Her husband's first and middle names are given in parentheses below her legal name.

31. An alphabetically arranged list of names illustrating many difficult points of alphabetizing follows.

COLUMN I	COLUMN II
Abbot , W.B.	54th St. Tailor Shop
Abbott, Alice	Forstall, W.J.
Allen, Alexander B.	44th St. Garage
Allen, Alexander B., Inc.	M A Delivery Co.
Andersen, Hans	M & C Amusement Corp.
Andersen, Hans E.	M C Art Assn.
Andersen, Hans E., Jr.	MacAdam, Wm.
Anderson, Andrew Andrews,	Macaulay, James
George Brown Motor Co., Boston	MacAulay, Wilson
Brown Motor Co., Chicago	MacDonald, R.J.
Brown Motor Co., Philadelphia	Macdonald, S.B.
Brown Motor Co., San Francisco	Mace, Wm.
Dean, Anna	Mazza, Anthony
Dean, Anna F.	McAdam, Wm.
Dean, Anna Frances	McAndrews, Jerry
Dean & Co.	Meade & Clark Co.
Deane-Arnold Apartments	Meade, S.T.
Deane's Pharmacy	Meade, Solomon
Deans, Felix A.	Sackett Publishing Co.
Dean's Studio	Sacks, Robert
Deans, Wm.	St.Andrew Hotel
Deans & Williams	St.John, Homer W.
East Randolph	Saks, Isaac B.
East St.Louis	Stephens, Ira
Easton, Pa.	Stevens, Delevan
Eastport, Me.	Stevens, Delila

IV. OFFICIAL EXAMINATION DIRECTIONS AND RULES

   To preclude the possibility of conflicting or varying methods of filing, explicit directions and express rules are given to the candidate before he answers the filing questions on an examination.

   The most recent official directions and rules for the filing questions are given immediately hereafter.

OFFICIAL DIRECTIONS

Each of questions ... to ... consists of four(five)names. For each question, select the one of the four(five)names that should be first (second)(third)(last) if the four(five)names were arranged in alphabetical order in accordance with the rules for alphabetical filing given below. Read these rules carefully. Then, for each question, indicate in the correspondingly numbered row on the answer sheet the letter preceding the name that should be first(second)(third)(last) in alphabetical order.

OFFICIAL RULES FOR ALPHABETICAL FILING

Names of Individuals

1. The names of individuals are filed in strict alphabetical order, first according to the last name, then according to first name or initial, and, finally, according to middle name or initial. For example: William Jones precedes George Kirk and Arthur S. Blake precedes Charles M. Blake.

2. When the last names are identical, the one with an initial instead of a first name precedes the one "with a first name beginning with the same initial. For example: J.Green precedes Joseph Green.

3. When identical last names also have identical first names, the one without a middle name or initial precedes the one with a middle name or initial. For example:Robert Jackson precedes both Robert C.Jackson and Robert Chester Jackson.

4. When last names are identical and the first names are also identical, the one with a middle initial precedes the one with a middle name beginning with the same initial. For example: Peter A. Brown precedes Peter Alvin Brown.

5. Prefixes such as De, El, La, and Van are considered parts of the names they precede. For example:Wilfred DeWald precedes Alexander Duval.

6. Last names beginning with "Mac" or "Mc" are filed as spelled.

7. Abbreviated names are treated as if they were spelled out. For example: Jos. is filed as Joseph and Robt. is filed as Robert.

8. Titles and designations such as Dr. ,Mrs., Prof. are disregarded in filing.

Names of Business Organizations

1. The names of business organizations are filed exactly as written, except that an organization bearing the name of an individual is filed alphabetically according to the name of the individual in accordance with the rules for filing names of individuals given above. For example: Thomas Allison Machine Company precedes Northern Baking Company.

2. When numerals occur in a name, they are treated as if they were spelled out. For example: 6 stands for six and 4th stands for fourth.

3. When the following words occur in names, they are disregarded: the, of, and Sample: Choose the name that should be filed *third*.

(A) Fred Town	(2)	(C) D. Town	(1)
(B) Jack Towne	(3)	(D) Jack S.Towne	(4)

The numbers in parentheses indicate the proper alphabetical order in which these names should be filed. Since the name that should be filed <u>third</u> is Jack Towne, the answer is (B).

FILING

EXAMINATION SECTION
TEST 1

DIRECTIONS: Each question from 1 through 10 contains four names. For each question, choose the name that should be *FIRST* if the four names were arranged in alphabetical order in accordance with the Rules for Alphabetical Filing given before. Read these rules carefully. Then, for each question, print in the space at the right the letter before the name that should be *FIRST* in alphabetical order.

SAMPLE QUESTION
A. Jane Earl   (2)
B. James A. Earle   (4)
C. James Earl   (1)
D. J. Earle   (3)

The numbers in parentheses show the proper alphabetical order in which these names should be filed. Since the name that should be filed *FIRST* is James Earl, the answer to the sample question is C.

1. A. Majorca Leather Goods   1.____
    B. Robert Maiorca and Sons
    C. Maintenance Management Corp.
    D. Majestic Carpet Mills

2. A. Municipal Telephone Service   2.____
    B. Municipal Reference Library
    C. Municipal Credit Union
    D. Municipal Broadcasting System

3. A. Robert B. Pierce   B. R. Bruce Pierce   3.____
    C. Ronald Pierce   D. Robert Bruce Pierce

4. A. Four Seasons Sports Club   4.____
    B. 14 Street Shopping Center
    C. Forty Thieves Restaurant
    D. 42nd St. Theaters

5. A. Franco Franceschini   B. Amos Franchini   5.____
    C. Sandra Franceschia   D. Lilie Franchinesca

6. A. Chas. A. Levine   B. Kurt Levene   6.____
    C. Charles Levine   D. Kurt E. Levene

7. A. Prof. Geo. Kinkaid   B. Mr. Alan Kinkaid   7.____
    C. Dr. Albert A. Kinkade   D. Kincade Liquors Inc.

8. A. Department of Public Events
    B. Office of the Public Administrator
    C. Queensborough Public Library
    D. Department of Public Health

8.__

9. A. Martin Luther King, Jr. Towers
    B. Metro North Plaza
    C. Manhattanville Houses
    D. Marble Hill Houses

9.__

10. A. Dr. Arthur Davids
    B. The David Check Cashing Service
    C. A. C. Davidsen
    D. Milton Davidoff

10.__

KEY (CORRECT ANSWERS)

1. C
2. D
3. B
4. D
5. C

6. B
7. D
8. B
9. A
10. B

TEST 2

DIRECTIONS: Each of questions 1 to 10 consists of four names. For each question, select the one of the four names that should be *THIRD* if the four names were arranged in alphabetical order in accordance with the Rules of Alphabetical Filing given before. Read these rules carefully. Then, for each question, print in the space at the right the letter preceding the name that should be *THIRD* in alphabetical order.

SAMPLE QUESTION

A. Fred Town   (2)
B. Jack Towne   (3)
C. D. Town   (1)
D. Jack S. Towne   (4)

The numbers in parentheses indicate the proper alphabetical order in which these names should be filed. Since the name that should be filed *THIRD* is Jack Towne, the answer is B.

1. A. Herbert Restman   B. H. Restman   1.____
    C. Harry Restmore   D. H. Restmore

2. A. Martha Eastwood   B. Martha E. Eastwood   2.____
    C. Martha Edna Eastwood D. M. Eastwood

3. A. Timothy Macalan   B. Fred McAlden   3.____
    C. Thomas MacAllister   D. Mrs. Frank McAllen

4. A. Elm Trading Co.   4.____
    B. El Dorado Trucking Corp.
    C. James Eldred Jewelry Store
    D. Eldridge Printing, Inc.

5. A. Edward La Gabriel   B. Marie Doris Gabriel   5.____
    C. Marjorie N. Gabriel   D. Mrs. Marian Gabriel

6. A. Peter La Vance   B. George Van Meer   6.____
    C. Wallace De Vance   D. Leonard Vance

7. A. Fifth Avenue Book Shop   7.____
    B. Mr. Wm. A. Fifner
    C. 52nd Street Association
    D. Robert B. Fiffner

8. A. Dr. Chas. D. Peterson B. Miss Irene F. Petersen   8.____
    C. Lawrence E. Peterson   D. Prof. N. A. Petersen

9. A. 71st Street Theater   B. The Seven Seas Corp.   9.____
    C. 7th Ave. Service Co.   D. Walter R. Sevan and Co.

10. A.   Aerol Auto Body, Inc.
     B.   AAB Automotive Service Corp.
     C.   Acer Automotive
     D.   Alerte Automotive Corp.

10._

KEY (CORRECT ANSWERS)

1.	D
2.	B
3.	B
4.	D
5.	C
6.	D
7.	A
8.	A
9.	C
10.	A

TEST 3

DIRECTIONS: Same as for Test 2.

1. A. William Carver   B. Howard Cambell   1.____
    C. Arthur Chambers   D. Charles Banner

2. A. Paul Moore   B. William Moore   2.____
    C. Paul A. Moore   D. William Allen Moore

3. A. George Peters   B. Eric Petersen   3.____
    C. G. Peters   D. E. Petersen

4. A. Edward Hallam   B. Jos. Frank Hamilton   4.____
    C. Edward A. Hallam   D. Joseph F. Hamilton

5. A. Theodore Madison   B. Timothy McGill   5.____
    C. Thomas MacLane   D. Thomas A. Madison

6. A. William O'Hara   B. Arthur Gordon   6.____
    C. James DeGraff   D. Anne von Glatin

7. A. Charles Green   B. Chas. T. Greene   7.____
    C. Charles Thomas Greene   D. Wm. A. Greene

8. A. John Foss Insurance Co.   B. New World Stove Co.   8.____
    C. 14th Street Dress Shop   D. Arthur Stein Paper Co.

9. A. Gold Trucking Co.   B. B. 8th Ave. Garage   9.____
    C. The First National Bank   D. The Century Novelty Co.

10. A. F. L. Doskow   B. Natalie S. Doskow   10.____
    C. Samuel B. Doskow   D. Arthur G. Doskor

KEY (CORRECT ANSWERS)

1. A
2. B
3. D
4. D
5. D

6. A
7. C
8. B
9. C
10. B

TEST 4

DIRECTIONS: Each question from 1 through 10 consists of four names. For each question, choose the one of the four names that should be *LAST* if the four names were arranged in alphabetical order in accordance with the Rules for Alphabetical Filing given before. Read these rules carefully. Then, for each question, print in the space at the right the letter before the name that should be *LAST* in alphabetical order.

SAMPLE QUESTION

A. Jane Earl (2)
B. James A. Earle (4)
C. James Earl (1)
D. J. Earle (3)

The numbers in parentheses show the proper alphabetical order in which these names should be filed. Since the name that should be filed *LAST* is James A. Earle, the answer to the sample question is B.

1.   A. Corral, Dr. Robert   B. Carrale, Prof. Robert   1.__
       C. Corren, R.   D. Corret, Ron

2.   A. Rivera, Ilena   B. Riviera, Ilene   2.__
       C. Rivere, I.   D. Riviera Ice-Cream Co.

3.   A. VonHogel, George   B. Volper, Gary   3.__
       C. Vonner, G.   D. Van Pefel, Gregory

4.   A. David Kallish Stationery Co.   4.__
       B. Emerson Microfilm Company
       C. David Kalder Industrial Engineers Associated
       D. 5th Avenue Office Furniture Co.

5.   A. A. Bennet, C.   B. Benett, Chuck   5.__
       C. Bennet, Chas.   D. Bennett, Charles

6.   A. The Board of Higher Education   6.__
       B. National Education Commission
       C. Eakin, Hugh
       D. Nathan, Ellen

7.   A. McCloud, I.   B. MacGowen, Ian   7.__
       C. McGowen, Arthur   D. Macale, Sean

8.   A. Devine, Sarah   B. Devine, S.   8.__
       C. Devine, Sara H.   D. Devin, Sarah

9.   A. Milstein, Louis   B. Milrad, Abraham P.   9.__
       C. Milstein, Herman   D. Milstien, Harold G.

10.   A. Herfield, Lester L.   B. Herbstman, Nathan   10.__
       C. Henricksen, Ole A.   D. Herfeld, Burton G.

KEY (CORRECT ANSWERS)

1. D
2. B
3. C
4. A
5. D

6. B
7. C
8. A
9. D
10. A

TEST 5

DIRECTIONS: Same as for Test 4.

1. A. Francis Lattimore   B. H. Latham   1.__
    C. G. Lattimore   D. Hugh Latham

2. A. Thomas B. Morgan   B. B. Thomas Morgan   2.__
    C. T. Morgan   D. Thomas Bertram Morgan

3. A. Lawrence A. Villon   B. Chas. Valente   3.__
    C. Charles M. Valent   D. Lawrence De Villon

4. A. Alfred Devance   B. A. R. D'Amico   4.__
    C. Arnold De Vincent   D. A. De Pino

5. A. Dr. Milton A. Bergmann   B. Miss Evelyn M. Bergmenn   5.__
    C. Prof. E. N. Bergmenn   D. Mrs. L. B. Bergmann

6. A. George MacDougald   B. Thomas McHern   6.__
    C. William Macholt   D. Frank McHenry

7. A. Third National Bank   B. Robt. Tempkin Corp.   7.__
    C. 32nd Street Carpet Co.   D. Wm. Templeton, Inc.

8. A. Mary Lobell Art Shop   B. John La Marca, Inc   8.__
    C. Lawyers' Guild   D. Frank Le Goff Studios

9. A. 9th Avenue Garage   B. Jos. Nuren Food Co.   9.__
    C. The New Book Store   D. Novelty Card Corp.

10. A. Murphy's Moving & Storage, Inc.   10.__
    B. Mid-Island Van Lines Corporation
    C. Mollone Bros. Moving & Storage, Inc.
    D. McShane Moving & Storage, Inc.

KEY (CORRECT ANSWERS)

1. C
2. D
3. A
4. C
5. B

6. B
7. C
8. A
9. B
10. A

TEST 6

DIRECTIONS: Each question contains four names numbered from 1 through 4 but not necessarily numbered in correct filing order. Answer each question by choosing the letter corresponding to the *CORRECT* filing order of the four names in accordance with the Rules for Alphabetic Filing given before. *PRINT THE LETTER OF THE CORRECT ANSWER IN THE SPACE AT THE RIGHT.*

SAMPLE QUESTION

1. Robert J. Smith
3. Dr. A. Smythe
2. R. Jeffrey Smith
4. Allen R. Smithers

A. 1, 2, 3, 4   B. 3, 1, 2, 4   C. 2, 1, 4, 3   D. 3, 2, 1, 4

Since the correct filing order, in accordance with the above rules, is 2, 1, 4, 3, the correct answer is C.

1. 1. J. Chester VanClief
   3. J. VanCleve
   2. John C. VanClief
   4. Mary L. Vance

   A. 4, 3, 1, 2   B. 4, 3, 2, 1   C. 3, 1, 2, 4   D. 3, 4, 1, 2   1.____

2. 1. Community Development Agency
   2. Department of Social Services
   3. Board of Estimate
   4. Bureau of Gas and Electricity   2.____

   A. 3, 4, 1, 2   B. 1, 2, 4, 3   C. 2, 1, 3, 4   D. 1, 3, 4, 2

3. 1. Dr. Chas. K. Dahlman
   3. Department of Water Supply
   2. F. & A. Delivery Service
   4. Demano Men's Custom Tailors   3.____

   A. 1, 2, 3, 4   B. 1, 4, 2, 3   C. 4, 1, 2, 3   D. 4, 1, 3, 2

4. 1. 48th Street Theater
   2. Fourteenth Street Day Care Center
   3. Professor A. Cartwright
   4. Albert F. McCarthy   4.____

   A. 4, 2, 1, 3   B. 4, 3, 1, 2   C. 3, 2, 1, 4   D. 3, 1, 2, 4

5. 1. Frances D'Arcy
   3. William H. Diamond
   2. Mario L. DelAmato
   4. Robert J. DuBarry   5.____

   A. 1, 2, 4, 3   B. 2, 1, 3, 4   C. 1, 2, 3, 4   D. 2, 1, 3, 4

6. 1. Evelyn H. D'Amelio
   3. Robert Bailey
   2. Jane R. Bailey
   4. Frank Baily   6.____

   A. 1, 2, 3, 4   B. 1, 3, 2, 4   C. 2, 3, 4, 1   D. 3, 2, 4, 1

7. 1. Department of Markets
   2. Bureau of Handicapped Children
   3. Housing Authority Administration Building
   4. Board of Pharmacy   7.____

A. 2,1,3,4   B. 1,2,4,3   C. 1,2,3,4   D. 3,2,1,4

8.   1.   William A. Shea Stadium   8.___
        2.   Rapid Speed Taxi Co.
        3.   Harry Stampler's Rotisserie
        4.   Wilhelm Albert Shea

        A. 2, 3, 4, 1   B. 4, 1, 3, 2   C. 2, 4, 1, 3   D. 3, 4, 1, 2

9.   1.   Robert S. Aaron, M. D.   2.   Mrs. Norma S. Aaron   9.___
        3.   Irving I. Aronson   4.   Darius P. Aanonsen

        A. 1, 2, 3, 4   B. 2, 4, 1, 3   C. 4, 2, 3, 1   D. 4, 2, 1, 3

10.   1.   The Gamut   2.   Gilliar Drug Co., Inc.   10.___
        3.   Georgette Cosmetology   4.   Great Nock Pharmacy

        A. 1, 3, 2, 4   B. 3, 1, 4, 2   C. 1, 2, 3, 4   D. 1, 3, 4, 2

KEY (CORRECT ANSWERS)

1.   A
2.   D
3.   B
4.   D
5.   C

6.   D
7.   D
8.   C
9.   D
10. A

TEST 7

DIRECTIONS: Each question consists of four names grouped vertically under four different filing arrangements lettered A, B, C, and D. In each question only one of the four arrangements lists the names in the correct filing order according to the Rules for Alphabetical Filing given before. Read these rules carefully. Then, for each question, select the correct filing arrangement, lettered A, B, C, or D and print in the space at the right the letter of that correct filing arrangement.

SAMPLE QUESTION

Arrangement A	*Arrangement B*	*Arrangement C*	*Arrangement D*
Arnold Robinson	Arthur Roberts	Arnold Robinson	Arthur Roberts
Arthur Roberts	J. B. Robin	Arthur Roberts	James Robin
J. B. Robin	James Robin	James Robin	J. B. Robin
James Robin	Arnold Robinson	J. B. Robin	Arnold Robinson

Since, in this sample, *ARRANGEMENT B* is the only one in which the four names are correctly arranged alphabetically, the answer is B.

1. *Arrangement A*
   Alice Thompson
   Arnold G. Thomas
   B. Thomas
   Eugene Thompkins
   Arrangement C
   B. Thomas Arnold
   G. Thomas
   Eugene Thompkins
   Alice Thompson

   Arrangement B
   Eugene Thompkins
   Alice Thompson
   Arnold G. Thomas
   B. Thomas
   Arrangement D
   Arnold G. Thomas
   B. Thomas
   Eugene Thompkins
   Alice Thompson

   1.____

2. *Arrangement A*
   Albert Green
   A. B. Green
   Frank E. Green
   Wm. Greenfield
   Arrangement C
   Albert Green
   Wm. Greenfield
   A. B. Green
   Frank E. Green

   Arrangement B
   A. B. Green
   Albert Green
   Frank E. Green
   Wm. Greenfield
   Arrangement D
   A. B. Green
   Frank E. Green
   Albert Green
   Wm. Greenfield

   2.____

3. *Arrangement A*
   Steven M. Comte
   Robt. Count
   Robert B. Count
   Steven Le Comte
   Arrangement C
   Steven M. Comte
   Steven Le Comte
   Robt. Count
   Robert B. Count

   Arrangement B
   Steven Le Comte
   Steven M. Comte
   Robert B. Count
   Robt. Count
   Arrangement D
   Robt. Count
   Robert B. Count
   Steven Le Comte
   Steven M. Comte

   3.____

4. *Arrangement A*
   Prof. David Towner
   Miss Edna Tower
   Dr. Frank I. Tower
   Mrs. K. C. Towner
   Arrangement C
   Miss Edna Tower
   Dr. Frank I. Tower
   Prof. David Towner
   Mrs. K. C. Towner

   Arrangement B
   Dr. Frank I. Tower
   Miss Edna Tower
   Mrs. K. C. Towner
   Prof. David Towner
   Arrangement D
   Prof. David Towner
   Mrs. K. C. Towner
   Miss Edna Tower
   Dr. Frank I. Tower

   4._

5. *Arrangement A*
   The Jane Miller Shop
   Joseph Millard Corp.
   John Muller & Co.
   Jean Mullins, Inc.
   Arrangement C
   The Jane Miller Shop
   Jean Mullins, Inc.
   John Muller & Co.
   Joseph Millard Corp.

   Arrangement B
   Joseph Millard Corp.
   The Jane Miller Shop
   John Muller & Co.
   Jean Mullins, Inc.
   Arrangement D
   Joseph Millard Corp.
   John Muller & Co.
   Jean Mullins, Inc.
   The Jane Miller Shop

   5._

6. *Arrangement A*
   Anthony Delaney
   A. M. D'Elia
   A. De Landri
   Alfred De Monte
   Arrangement C
   A. De Landri
   A. M. D'Elia
   Alfred De Monte
   Anthony Delaney

   Arrangement B
   Anthony Delaney
   A. De Landri
   A. M. D'Elia
   Alfred De Monte
   Arrangement D
   A. De Landri
   Anthony Delaney
   A. M. D'Elia
   Alfred De Monte

   6._

7. *Arrangement A*
   D. McAllen
   Lewis McBride
   Doris MacAllister
   Lewis T. Mac Bride
   Arrangement C
   Doris MacAllister
   Lewis T. MacBride
   D. McAllen
   Lewis McBride

   Arrangement B
   D. McAllen
   Doris MacAllister
   Lewis McBride
   Lewis T. MacBride
   Arrangement D
   Doris MacAllister
   D. McAllen
   Lewis T. MacBride
   Lewis McBride

   7._

8. *Arrangement A*
   6th Ave. Swim Shop
   The Sky Ski School
   Sport Shoe Store
   23rd Street Salon
   Arrangement C
   6th Ave. Swim Shop
   Sport Shoe Store
   The Sky Ski School
   23rd Street Salon

   Arrangement B
   23rd Street Salon
   The Sky Ski School
   6th Ave. Swim Shop
   Sport Shoe Store
   Arrangement D
   The Sky Ski School
   6th Ave. Swim Shop
   Sport Shoe Store
   23rd Street Salon

   8.____

9. *Arrangement A*
   Charlotte Stair
   C. B. Stare
   Charles B. Stare
   Elaine La Stella
   Arrangement C
   Elaine La Stella
   Charlotte Stair
   C. B. Stare
   Charles B. Stare

   Arrangement B
   C. B. Stare
   Charles B. Stare
   Charlotte Stair
   Elaine La Stella
   Arrangement D
   Charles B. Stare
   C. B. Stare
   Charlotte Stair
   Elaine La Stella

   9.____

10. *Arrangement A*
    John O'Farrell Corp.
    Finest Glass Co.
    George Fraser Co.
    4th Guarantee Bank
    Arrangement C
    John O'Farrell Corp.
    Finest Glass Co.
    4th Guarantee Bank
    George Fraser Co.

    Arrangement B
    Finest Glass Co.
    4th Guarantee Bank
    George Fraser Co.
    John O'Farrell Corp.
    Arrangement D
    Finest Glass Co.
    George Fraser Co.
    John O'Farrell Corp.
    4th Guarantee Bank

    10.____

KEY (CORRECT ANSWERS)

1. D
2. B
3. A
4. C
5. B

6. D
7. C
8. A
9. C
10. B

TEST 8

DIRECTIONS: Same as for Test 7.

Arrangement A	Arrangement B	Arrangement C	
1. R. B. Stevens Chas. Stevenson Robert Stevens,Sr. Alfred T. Stevens	Alfred T. Stevens R. B. Stevens Robert Stevens,Sr. Chas. Stevenson	R. B. Stevens Robert Stevens,Sr. Alfred T. Stevens Chas. Stevenson	1.＿
2. Mr. A. T. Breen Dr. Otis C. Breen Amelia K.Brewington John Brewington	John Brewington Amelia K.Brewington Dr. Otis C. Breen Mr. A. T. Breen	Dr. Otis C. Breen Mr. A. T. Breen John Brewington Amelia K.Brewington	2.＿
3. J. Murphy J. J. Murphy John Murphy John J. Murphy	John Murphy John J. Murphy J. Murphy J. J. Murphy	J. Murphy John Murphy J. J. Murphy John J. Murphy	3.＿
4. Anthony DiBuono George Burns,Sr. Geo. T. Burns,Jr. Alan J. Byrnes	Geo. T. Burns,Jr. George Burns,Sr. Anthony DiBuono Alan J. Byrnes	George Burns,Sr. Geo. T. Burns, Jr. Alan J. Byrnes Anthony DiBuono	4.＿
5. James Macauley Frank A. McLowery Francis MacLaughry Bernard J. MacMahon	James Macauley Francis MacLoughry Bernard J. MacMahon Frank A. McLowery	Bernard J. MacMahon Francis MacLaughry Frank A. McLowery James Macauley	5.＿
6. A.J. DiBartolo,Sr. A. P. DiBartolo J. A. Bartolo Anthony J. Bartolo	J. A. Bartolo Anthony J. Bartolo A. P. DiBartolo A. J. DiBartolo,Sr.	Anthony J. Bartolo J. A. Bartolo A. J. DiBartolo, Sr. A. P. DiBartolo	6.＿
7. Edward Holmes Corp. Hillside Trust Corp Standard Insurance Co. The Industrial Surety Co.	Edward Holmes Corp. Hillside Trust Corp. The Industrial Surety Co. Standard Insurance Co.	Hillside TrustCorp. Edward Holmes Corp. The Industrial Surety Co. Standard InsuranceCo.	7.＿
8. Cooperative Credit Co. Chas. Cooke Chemical Corp. John Fuller Baking Co. 4th Avenue Express Co.	Chas. Cooke Chemical Corp. Cooperative Credit Co. 4th Avenue Express Co. John Fuller Baking Co.	4th Avenue Express Co. John Fuller Baking Co. Chas. Cooke Chemical Corp. Cooperative CreditCo.	8.＿

9. Mr. R. McDaniels
Robert Darling, Jr.
F. L. Ramsey
Charles DeRhone

F. L. Ramsey
Mr. R. McDaniels
Charles DeRhone
Robert Darling, Jr.

Robert Darling, Jr. Charles
DeRhone
Mr. R. McDaniels
F. L. Ramsey

9.____

10. New York Omnibus Corp.
New York Shipping Co.
Nova Scotia Canning Co.
John J. O'Brien Co.

John J. O'Brien Co.
New York Omnibus Corp.
New York Shipping Co.
Nova Scotia Caning Co.

Nova Scotia Canning Co.
John J. O'Brien Co.
New York Omnibus Corp.
New York Shipping Co.

10.____

KEY (CORRECT ANSWERS)

1. B
2. A
3. A
4. C
5. B

6. C
7. C
8. B
9. C
10. A

TEST 9

DIRECTIONS: Each question consists of a group of names. Consider each group of names as a unit. Determine in what position the name printed in *ITALICS* would be if the names in the group were *CORRECTLY* arranged in alphabetical order. If the name in *ITALICS* should be first, print the letter A; if second, print the letter B; if third, print the letter C; if fourth, print the letter D; and if fifth, print the letter E. *PRINT THE LETTER OF THE CORRECT ANSWER IN THE SPACE AT THE RIGHT.*

SAMPLE QUESTION

J. W. Martin	2
James E. Martin	4
J. Martin	1
George Martins	5
James Martin	3

1. Albert Brown
    James Borenstein
    Frieda Albrecht
    Samuel Brown
    George Appelman

    1.___

2. James Ryan
    Francis Ryan
    Wm. Roanan
    Frances S. Ryan
    Francis P. Ryan

    2.___

3. Norman Fitzgibbons
    Charles F. Franklin
    Jas. Fitzgerald
    Andrew Fitzsimmons
    James P. Fitzgerald

    3.___

4. Hugh F. Martenson
    A. S. Martinson
    Albert Martinsen
    Albert S. Martinson
    M. Martanson

    4.___

5. Aaron M. Michelson
    Samuel Michels
    Arthur L. Michaelson, Sr.
    John Michell
    Daniel Michelsohn

    5.___

6. *Chas. R. Connolly*
    Frank Conlon
    Charles S. Connolly
    Abraham Cohen
    Chas. Conolly

6._____

7. James McCormack
    Ruth MacNamara
    Kathryn McGillicuddy
    Frances Mason
    Arthur MacAdams

7._____

8. Dr. Francis Karell
    John Joseph Karelsen,
    Jr. John J.Karelsen,Sr.
    Mrs. Jeanette Kelly
    Estelle Karel

8._____

9. *The 5th Ave. Bus Co.*
    The Baltimore and Ohio Railroad
    3rd Ave. Elevated Co.
    Pennsylvania Railroad
    The 4th Ave. Trolley Line

9._____

10. Murray B. Cunitz
    Cunningham Duct Cleaning Corp.
    James A. Cunninghame
    Jason M. Cuomor
    Talmadge L. Cummings

10._____

KEY (CORRECT ANSWERS)

1.	E
2.	D
3.	A
4.	E
5.	D
6.	C
7.	C
8.	D
9.	B
10.	C

TEST 10

DIRECTIONS: A supervisor who is responsible for the proper maintenance and operation of the filing system in an office of a depart-ment should be able to instruct and guide his subordinates in the correct filing of office records. The following ques-tions,1 through 10, are designed to determine whether you can interpret and follow a prescribed filing procedure. These questions should be answered SOLELY on the basis of the fil-ing instructions which follow.

FILING INSTRUCTIONS FOR PERSONNEL DIVISION
DEPARTMENT X

The filing system of this division consists of three separate files, namely: (1) Employee File, (2) Subject File, (3) Correspondence File.

Employee File

This file contains a folder for each person currently employed in the department. Each report, memorandum, and letter which has been received from an official or employee of the department and which pertions to one employee only should be placed in the Employee File folder of the employee with whom the communication is concerned. (Note: This filing proce-dure also applies to a communication from a staff member who writes on a matter which con-cerns himself only.)

Subject File

Reports and memoranda originating in the department and dealing with personnel mat-ters affecting the entire staff or certain categories or groups of employees should be placed in the Subject File under the appropriate subject headings. The materials in this file are subdi-vided under the following five subject headings:

(1) Classification -- includes material on job analysis, change of title, reclassifica-tion of positions, etc.

(2) Employment -- includes material on appointment, promotion, re-instatement, and transfer.

(3) Health and Safety -- includes material dealing chiefly with the health and safety of employees.

(4) Staff Regulations -- includes material pertaining to rules and regulations gov-erning such working conditions as hours of work, lateness, vacation, leave of absence, etc.

(5) Training -- includes all material relating to employee training.

Correspondence File

All correspondence received from outside agencies, both public and private, and from persons outside the department, should be placed in the Correspondence File and cross ref-erenced as follows:

(1) When letters from outside agencies or persons relate to one or more employees currently employed in the department, a cross reference sheet should be placed in the Employee File folder of each employee mentioned.

(2) When letters from outside agencies or persons do not mention a specific employee or specific employees of the department, a cross reference sheet should be placed in the Subject File under the appropriate subject heading.

Questions 1-10 describe communications which have been received and acted upon by the Personnel Division of Department X, and which must be filed in accordance with the Filing Instructions for the Personnel Division.

The following filing operations may be performed in accordance with the above filing instructions:

- (A)　Place in Employee File
- (B)　Place in Subject File under Classification
- (C)　Place in Subject File tinder Employment
- (D)　Place in Subject File under Health and Safety
- (E)　Place in Subject File under Staff Regulations
- (F)　Place in Subject File under Training
- (G)　Place in Correspondence File and cross reference in Employee File
- (H)　Place in Correspondence File and cross reference in Subject File under Classification
- (I)　Place in Correspondence File and cross reference in Subject File under Employment
- (J)　Place in Correspondence File and cross reference in Subject File under Health and Safety
- (K)　Place in Correspondence File and cross reference in Subject File under Staff Regulations
- (L)　Place in Correspondence File and cross reference in Subject File under Training

DIRECTIONS:　Examine each of questions 1 through 10 carefully. Then, in the space at the right, *print* the capital letter preceding the one of the filing operations listed above which MOST accurately carries out the Filing Instructions for the Personnel Division.

SAMPLE:　A Clerk, Grade 2, in the department has sent in a memorandum requesting information regarding the amount of vacation due him.
The CORRECT answer is A.

1. Mr. Clark, a Clerk, Grade 5, has submitted an intradepartmental memorandum that the titles of all Clerks, Grade 5, in the department be changed to Administrative Assistant.

1.＿＿＿＿

2. The secretary to the department has issued a staff order revising the schedule of Saturday work from a one-in-two to a one-in-four schedule.

2.＿＿＿＿

3. The personnel officer of another agency has requested the printed transcripts of an in-service course recently conducted by the department.

3.＿＿＿＿

4. Mary Smith, a secretary to one of the division chiefs, has sent in a request for a maternity leave of absence to begin on April 1 of this year and to terminate on March 31 of next year.

4.＿＿＿＿

5. A letter has been received from a civic organization stating that they would like to know how many employees were promoted in the department during the last fiscal year.

5.＿＿＿＿

6. The attorney for a municipal employees' organization has requested permission to represent Mr.James Roe, a departmental employee who is being brought up on charges of violating departmental regulations.

6.＿＿＿＿

7. A letter has been received from Mr. Wright, a salesman for a paper company, who complains that Miss Jones, an information clerk in the department, has been rude and impertinent and has refused to give him information which should be available to the public.

7.＿＿＿＿

8. Helen Brown, a graduate of Commercial High School, has sent a letter inquiring about an appointment as a provisional typist. 8.__

9. The National Office Managers' Society has sent a request to the department for information on its policies on tardiness and absenteeism. 9.__

10. A memorandum has been received from a division chief who states that employees in his unit have complained that their rest room is in a very unsanitary condition. 10.__

KEY (CORRECT ANSWERS)

1. B
2. E
3. L
4. A
5. I

6. G
7. G
8. I
9. K
10. D

NAME AND NUMBER CHECKING

EXAMINATION SECTION
TEST 1

DIRECTIONS: This test is designed to measure your speed and accuracy. You are urged to work both quickly and accurately and to do correctly as many lists as you can in the time allowed. The test consists of lists of pairs of names and numbers. Count the number of IDENTICAL pairs in each list. Then, select the correct number, 1, 2, 3, 4, or 5, and indicate your choice by circling the corresponding number on your answer paper, Two sample questions are presented for your guidance, together with the correct solutions.

SAMPLE QUESTIONS

SAMPLE LIST A

		CIRCLE CORRECT ANSWER
Adelphi College	- Adelphia College	1 2 3 4 5
Braxton Corp.	- Braxeton Corp.	
Wassaic State School	- Wassaic State School	
Central Islip State Hospital	- Central Isllip State	
Greenwich House	- Greenwich House	

NOTE that there are only two correct pairs - Wassaic State School and Greenwich House. Therefore, the CORRECT answer is 2.

SAMPLE LIST B

78453694	- 78453684	1 2 3 4 5
784530	- 784530	
533	- 534	
67845	- 67845	
2368745	- 2368755	

NOTE that there are only two correct pairs - 784530 and 67845. Therefore, the COR-RECT answer is 2.

LIST 1

98654327	- 98654327	1 2 3 4 5
74932564	- 74922564	
61438652	- 61438652	
01297653	- 01287653	
1865439765	- 1865439765	

LIST 2

478362	- 478363	1 2 3 4 5
278354792	- 278354772	
9327	- 9327	
297384625	- 27384625	
6428156	- 6428158	

LIST 3

		CIRCLE

Abbey House   - Abbey House

Actors' Fund Home   - Actor's Fund Home

Adrian Memorial   - Adrian Memorial

A. Clayton Powell Home   - Clayton Powell House

Abott E. Kittredge Club   - Abbott E. Kitteredge Club

CIRCLE CORRECT ANSWER   1   2   3   4   5

LIST 4

3682   - 3692

21937453829   - 31937453829

723   - 733

2763920   - 2763920

47293   - 47293

1   2   3   4   5

LIST 5

Adra House   - Adra House

Adolescents' Court   - Adolescents' Court

Cliff Villa   - Cliff Villa

Clark Neighborhood House   - Clark Neighborhood House

Alma Mathews House   - Alma Mathews House

1   2   3   4   5

LIST 6

28734291   - 28734271

63810263849   - 63810263846

26831027   - 26831027

368291   - 368291

7238102637   - 7238102637

1   2   3   4   5

LIST 7

Albion State T.S.   - Albion State T.C.

Clara de Hirsch Home   - Clara De Hirsch Home

Alice Carrington Royce   - Alice Carington Royce

Alice Chopin Nursery   - Alice Chapin Nursery

Lighthouse Eye Clinic   - Lighthouse Eye Clinic

1   2   3   4   5

LIST 8

327   - 329

712438291026   - 712438291026

2753829142   - 275382942

826287   - 826289

26435162839   - 26435162839

1   2   3   4   5

LIST 9

Letchworth Village   - Letchworth Village

A.A.A.E. Inc.   - A.A.A.E. Inc.

Clear Pool Camp   - Clear Pool Camp

A.M.M.L.A. Inc.   - A.M.M.L.A. Inc.

J.G. Harbard   - J.G. Harbord

1   2   3   4   5

CIRCLE
CORRECT ANSWER

LIST 10

| | | 1 2 3 4 5 |

8254 - 8256
2641526 - 2641526
4126389012 - 4126389102
725 - 725
76253917287 - 76253917287

1 2 3 4 5

LIST 11

Attica State Prison - Attica State Prison
Nellie Murrah - Nellie Murrah
Club Marshall - Club Marshal
Assissium Casea-Maria - Assissium Casa-Maria
The Homestead - The Homestead

1 2 3 4 5

LIST 12

2691 - 2691
623819253627 - 623819253629
28637 - 28937
278392736 - 278392736
52739 - 52739

1 2 3 4 5

LIST 13

A.I.C.P. Boys Camp - A.I.C.P. Boy's Camp
Einar Chrystie - Einar Christyie
Astoria Center - Astoria Center
G. Frederick Brown - G. Federick Browne
Vacation Service - Vacation Services

1 2 3 4 5

LIST 14

728352689 - 728352688
643728 - 643728
37829176 - 37827196
8425367 - 8425369
65382018 - 65382018

1 2 3 4 5

LIST 15

E.S. Streim - E.S. Strim
Charles E. Higgins - Charles E. Higgins
Baluvelt, N.Y. - Blauwelt, N.Y.
Roberta Magdalen - Roberto Magdalen
Ballard School - Ballard School

1 2 3 4 5

LIST 16

7382 - 7392
281374538299 - 291374538299
623 - 633
6273730 - 6273730
63392 - 63392

LIST 17

Orrin Otis	- Orrin Otis	1 2 3 4 5
Barat Settlement	- Barat Settlemen	
Emmanuel House	- Emmanuel House	
William T. McCreery	- William T. McCreery	
Seamen's Home	- Seaman's Home	

LIST 18

72824391	- 72834371	1 2 3 4 5
3729106237	- 37291106237	
82620163849	- 82620163846	
37638921	- 37638921	
82631027	- 82631027	

LIST 19

Commonwealth Fund	- Commonwealth Fund	1 2 3 4 5
Anne Johnsen	- Anne Johnson	
Bide-a-Wee Home	- Bide-a-Wee Home	
Riverdale-on-Hudson	- Riverdal-on-Hudson	
Bialystoker Home	- Bailystoker Home	

LIST 20

9271	- 9271	1 2 3 4 5
392918352627	- 392018852629	
72637	- 72637	
927392736	- 927392736	
92739	- 92739	

LIST 21

Charles M. Stump	- Charles M. Stump	1 2 3 4 5
Bourne Workshop	- Buorne Workshop	
B'nai Bi'rith	- B'nai Brith	
Poppenhuesen Institute	- Poppenheusen Institute	
Consular Service	- Consular Service	

LIST 22

927352689	- 927352688	1 2 3 4 5
647382	- 648382	
93729176	- 93727196	
649536718	- 649536718	
5835367	- 5835369	

LIST 23

L.S. Bestend	- L.S. Bestent	1 2 3 4 5
Hirsch Mfg. Co.	- Hircsh Mfg. Co.	
F.H. Storrs	- F.P. Storrs	
Camp Wassaic	- Camp Wassaic	
George Ballingham	- George Ballingham	

LIST 24

372846392048	- 372846392048
334	- 334
7283524678	- 7283524678
7283	- 7283
7283629372	- 7283629372

CIRCLE
CORRECT ANSWER
1 2 3 4 5

LIST 25

Dr. Stiles Company	- Dr. Stills Company
Frances Hunsdon	- Frances Hunsdon
Northrop Barrert	- Nothrup Barrent
J. D. Brunjes	- J. D. Brunjes
Theo. Claudel & Co.	- Theo. Claudel co.

1 2 3 4 5

KEY (CORRECT ANSWERS)

1.	3		11.	3
2.	1		12.	3
3.	2		13.	1
4.	2		14.	2
5.	5		15.	2
6.	3		16.	2
7.	1		17.	3
8.	2		18.	2
9.	4		19.	2
10.	3		20.	4

21.	2
22.	1
23.	2
24.	5
25.	2

TEST 2

DIRECTIONS: This test is designed to measure your speed and accuracy. You are urged to work both quickly and accurately and to do correctly as many lists as you can in the time allowed. The test consists of lists of pairs of names and numbers. Count the number of IDENTICAL pairs in each list. Then, select the correct number, 1, 2, 3, 4, or 5, and indicate your choice by circling the corresponding number on your answer paper, Two sample questions are presented for your guidance, together with the correct solutions.

LIST 1

82728	- 82738	CIRCLE
82736292637	- 82736292639	CORRECT ANSWER
728	- 738	1 2 3 4 5
83926192527	- 83726192529	
82736272	- 82736272	

LIST 2

L. Pietri	- L. Pietri	
Mathewson, L.F.	- Mathewson, L.F.	
Funk & Wagnall	- Funk & Wagnalls	1 2 3 4 5
Shimizu, Sojio	- Shimizu, Sojio	
Filing Equipment Bureau	- Filing Equipment Buraeu	

LIST 3

63801829374	- 63801839474	
283577657	- 283577657	
65689	- 65689	1 2 3 4 5
3457892026	- 3547893026	
2779	- 2778	

LIST 4

August Caille	- August Caille	
The Well-Fare Service	- The Wel-Fare Service	
K.L.M. Process Co.	- R.L.M. Process Co.	1 2 3 4 5
Merrill Littell	- Merrill Littell	
Dodd & Sons	- Dodd & Son	

LIST 5

998745732	- 998745733	
723	- 723	
463849102983	- 463849102983	1 2 3 4 5
8570	- 8570	
279012	- 279012	

LIST 6

M. A. Wender	- M.A. Winder	
Minneapolis Supply Co.	- Minneapolis Supply Co.	
Beverly Hills Corp	- Beverley Hills Corp.	1 2 3 4 5
Trafalgar Square	- Trafalgar Square	
Phifer, D.T.	- Phiefer, D.T.	

LIST 7
7834629	- 7834629
3549806746	- 3549806746
97802564	- 97892564
689246	- 688246
2578024683	- 2578024683

1 2 3 4 5

LIST 8
Scadrons'	- Scadrons'
Gensen & Bro.	- Genson & Bro.
Firestone Co.	- Firestone Co.
H.L. Eklund ·	- H.L. Eklund
Oleomargarine Co.	- Oleomargarine Co.

1 2 3 4 5

LIST 9
782039485618	- 782039485618
53829172639	- 63829172639
892	- 892
82937482	- 829374820
52937456	- 53937456

1 2 3 4 5

LIST 10
First Nat'l Bank	- First Nat'l Bank
Sedgwick Machine Works	- Sedgewick Machine Works
Hectographia Co.	- Hectographia Corp.
Levet Bros.	- Levet Bros.
Multistamp Co.,Inc.	- Multistamp Co.,Inc.

1 2 3 4 5

LIST 11
7293	- 7293
6382910293	- 6382910292
981928374012	- 981928374912
58293	- 58393
18203649271	- 283019283745

1 2 3 4 5

LIST 12
Lowrey Lb'r Co.	- Lowrey Lb'r Co.
Fidelity Service	- Fidelity Service
Reumann, J.A.	- Reumann, J.A.
Duophoto Ltd.	- Duophotos Ltd.
John Jarratt	- John Jaratt

1 2 3 4 5

LIST 13
6820384	- 6820384
383019283745	- 383019283745
63927102	- 63928102
91029354829	- 91029354829
58291728	- 58291728

1 2 3 4 5

LIST 14

Standard Press Co.	- Standard Press Co.	CIRCLE CORRECT ANSWER
Reliant Mf'g. Co.	- Relant Mf'g Co.	1 2 3 4 5
M.C. Lynn	- M.C. Lynn	
J. Fredericks Company	- G. Fredericks Company	
Wandermann, B.S.	- Wanderman, B.S.	

LIST 15

4283910293	- 4283010203	1 2 3 4 5
992018273648	- 992018273848	
620	- 629	
752937273	- 752937373	
5392	- 5392	

LIST 16

Waldorf Hotel	- Waldorf Hotel	1 2 3 4 5
Aaron Machinery Co.	- Aaron Machinery Co.	
Caroline Ann Locke	- Caroline Anne Locke	
McCabe Mfg. Co.	- McCabe Mfg. Co.	
R.L. Landres	- R.L. Landers	

LIST 17

68391028364	- 68391028394	1 2 3 4 5
68293	- 68293	
739201	- 739201	
72839201	- 72839211	
739917	- 739719	

LIST 18

Balsam M.M.	- Balsamm, M.M.	1 2 3 4 5
Steinway & Co.	- Stienway & M. Co.	
Eugene Elliott	- Eugene A. Elliott	
Leonard Loan Co.	- Leonard Loan Co.	
Frederick Morgan	- Frederick Morgen	

LIST 19

8929	- 9820	1 2 3 4 5
392836472829	- 392836472829	
462	- 462 2039271	
827	- 2039276837	
53829	- 54829	

LIST 20

Danielson's Hofbrau	- Danielson's Hafbrau	1 2 3 4 5
Edward A. Truarme	- Edward A. Truame	
Insulite Co.	- Insulite Co.	
Reisler Shoe Corp,	- Rielser Shoe Corp.	
L.L. Thompson	- L.L. Thompson	

LIST 21

92839102837	- 92839102837
58891028	- 58891028
7291728	- 7291928
272839102839	- 272839102839
428192	- 428102

1 2 3 4 5

LIST 22

K.L. Veiller	- K.L. Veiller
Webster, Roy	- Webster, Ray
Drasner Spring Co.	- Drasner Spring Co.
Edward J. Cravenport	- Edward J. Cravanport
Harold Field	- Harold A. Field

1 2 3 4 5

LIST 23

2293	- 2293
4283910293	- 5382910292
871928374012	- 871928374912
68293	- 68393
8120364927	- 81293649271

1 2 3 4 5

LIST 24

Tappe, Inc	- Tappe, Inc.
A.M. Wentingworth	- A.M. Wentinworth
Scott A. Elliott	- Scott A. Elliott
Echeverria Corp.	- Echeverria Corp.
Bradford Victor Company	- Bradford Victer Company

1 2 3 4 5

LIST 25

4820384	- 4820384
393019283745	- 283919283745
63927102	- 63927102
91029354829	- 91029354829
48291728	- 48291728

1 2 3 4 5

KEY (CORRECT ANSWERS)

1.	1		11.	1
2.	3		12.	3
3.	2		13.	4
4.	2		14.	2
5.	4		15.	1
6.	2		16.	3
7.	3		17.	2
8.	4		18.	1
9.	2		19.	1
10.	3		20.	2

21.	3
22.	2
23.	1
24.	2
25.	4

9 781731 867